Praise for

RADICAL

"When it comes to spinning light and shadow on the complexities of living, loving and language, Xiaolu Guo is one of the most valuable writers in the world." —**Deborah Levy, author of** *The Cost of Living*

"*Radical* is difficult to describe because it's difficult to categorize. It might be called a memoir, but its form makes it unlike any memoir readers may have encountered before." —**Shakespeare and Company**

"An elegant and unreserved account of a life lived in full recognition of its possibilities." —*Kirkus Reviews*

"A wild, passionate, gorgeous book, wandering the borders of language and desire; walking cities and remembering the ghosts of past landscapes. Xiaolu Guo's books always open up new connections and curiosities for me. She is certainly among my favourite contemporary writers." —**Ayşegül Savaş, author of** *White on White*

"[*Radical* is] an etymological exploration in search of a self-defined life . . . Guo has mastered the language in which she writes; here, she digs further through the layers of all her languages to reveal the life constructed by her own hands, in her own words . . . a visual exploration as well as a linguistic one." —**Nancy Seidler,** *Rain Taxi*

"An etymological voyage that lives up to its title: radical in angle of attack, smart and brave. Making the urban condition of restlessness and pain into poetry." —**Iain Sinclair, author of** *The Gold Machine*

"[A] fascinating memoir . . . Hyperliterate and formally inventive, this often exhilarating memoir lives up to its title and then some." —*Publishers Weekly*

"Xiaolu Guo is a writer like no other, and this is a memoir like no other. Organized through a series of words that cut across languages, the book shows the divides and the connections that define a life lived between China, Europe and America, all explained with wit, lightness of touch and the occasional pinch of heartbreak." —**Rana Mitter, Professor of the History and Politics of Modern China, University of Oxford**

RADICAL

ALSO BY XIAOLU GUO

Village of Stone

A Concise Chinese–English Dictionary for Lovers

Twenty Fragments of a Ravenous Youth

UFO in Her Eyes

Lovers in the Age of Indifference

I Am China

Nine Continents

A Lover's Discourse

RADICAL

A LIFE OF
MY OWN

XIAOLU GUO

Grove Press
New York

First published in the UK in 2023 by Chatto & Windus, an imprint of Vintage, part of the Penguin Random House group.

Simultaneously published in Canada
Printed in the United States of America

First Grove Atlantic hardcover edition: September 2023
First Grove Atlantic paperback edition: September 2024

Typeset in 10.6/14.5pt Minion Pro by Jouve (UK), Milton Keynes

Library of Congress Cataloging-in-Publication data is available for this title.

ISBN 978-0-8021-6359-2
eISBN 978-0-8021-6157-4

Grove Press
an imprint of Grove Atlantic
154 West 14th Street
New York, NY 10011

Distributed by Publishers Group West

groveatlantic.com

24 25 26 27 28 29   10 9 8 7 6 5 4 3 2 1

The limits of my language mean the limits of my world.

Ludwig Wittgenstein

A good traveller has no fixed plans, and is not intent on arriving.

Lao Tzu

Contents

头 / *Head*   *ix*

I. LEXICON OF ENCOUNTERS

1   栖 (dwell, residence, house)   3
2   女 (female, girl, woman)   31
3   言 (language, speech, words)   67
4   气 (qi, energy, spirit)   95
5   色 (sex, colour, beauty)   115

II. LEXICON OF SEPARATIONS

6   分 (separation, parting, disconnection)   129
7   木 (wood, root, plant)   149
8   疒 (malady, disease, disorder)   171
9   走 (walk, step, move)   185
10   身 (body, flesh, figure)   201
11   土 (earth, soil, land)   211

III. LEXICON OF ENDURING

12   音 (music, sound, melody)   233
13   辛 (endurance, bitterness, suffering)   251
14   生 (live, vigour, raw)   275

IV. LEXICON OF IMPERMANENCE

15   死 (death, killing, demise)   291
16   史 (history, past, saga)   309
17   未 (future, forthcoming, hereafter)   319

尾 / *Tail*   *331*
Notes and Bibliography   *333*
List of Artworks   *336*
Acknowledgements   *339*

头 / HEAD

Once Upon a Time / Jadis / Einst / Érase una vez / C'era una volta / 从前

Rimbaud's well-known poem 'A Season in Hell' begins: *Jadis, si je me souviens bien* . . . (Once, if I remember well . . .)

A long time ago, if I remember well, I spoke only a rural dialect, and I could not write. Then the dialect left me, or I abandoned it, because I turned to another.

If I remember well, I spoke that second dialect, and learned to write. I wrote ideograms – *hanzi*, as we say in China.

And, if I remember well, eventually I came to speak an official language, and wrote in that language too, and my second dialect retreated behind my tongue. But my memory kept the sounds and connotations of the old words, and my jaw and mouth moved in the old ways.

Then, I left the East for the West, and adopted yet another language. But my lips and jaw kept pulling my muscles back to the old movements, which made my speech sound alien – both to my own ears and to others. In that estrangement, I began to write. I wrote using an alphabet, not ideograms.

Since then, I have been separated from my original languages. I can say that I have a new language now, but I cannot say that it is my own.

To have a life of my own, is to have a language of my own. To make this language mine, I have to recover the languages I have lost, weave them into the present. An impossible task, perhaps. Still, here I am, in pursuit of an etymology of myself.

I

Lexicon of Encounters

1

Radical: 栖

(dwell, residence, house)

Radical

部首

A bushou is a radical, a Chinese pictogram that is a building block for more complex characters. Bushou are the roots from which all words grow and meanings bloom.

Writing systems in the West use alphabets. The Chinese language uses pictograms and ideograms. Alphabets are codes for sounds. Pictograms depict objects and impressions. The West writes symbolically, the Chinese writes visually.

Our Chinese ideograms are made up of *bushou*. *Bushou* can be translated as 'radical', meaning 'root' in Latin. But when you look at the word *bushou* it literally means parts and heads. *Bushou* are the organs of the bodies, through which we write. For example, 山 is the radical for mountain. If you put a man beside a mountain, it becomes a sage: 仙. And if you add the water symbol by the mountain, it becomes a dune: 汕. Our radicals are the parts and heads of the Chinese characters.

In English, 'radical' can be a noun or an adjective. It has other meanings: departure from tradition, or advocating great reforms. In Chinese that's a different word. It's *jijin* – 激进. *Jijin* has nothing to do with roots. It has to do with water rushing forward, just as progressive thinking bursts forth into the future.

However, in my mind 'radical' and 'bushou' are intertwined, they criss-cross. For me, many words are like this: the Chinese merges with the English. My linguistic life is a journey through this forest of entanglement, looking for a path. Many of the trees and plants in the forest are deeply familiar to me, others I have never climbed or touched. But no matter where I explore, I always want to keep contact with my roots, with my *bushou*, even when I find myself in an unknown wordscape.

Empire State Building
帝国大厦

A skyscraper on Fifth Avenue in Manhattan completed in the 1930s. For several decades it was the tallest building in the world.

I walked towards the Empire State Building in Midtown. Close to it but still on 32nd or 34th Street, I discovered that the edifice had disappeared. I raised my chin to the sky, spinning like a levitating top, but I couldn't locate the spire. The buildings I could see were equally immense, with art deco facades.  They encircled me in every direction. I knew I was only eighty or a hundred metres away from the Empire State Building but I had lost all sense of orientation.

Yes, once you get close to something, it disappears. It's like the idea of searching for ancient Japan after arriving at Tokyo airport, or trying to locate an idyllic village hidden at the foot of a Basque mountain. It does not belong to reality. The Empire State Building appears to exist only in thin air, in the ever expanding distance. It is more an idea than a material thing. The closer you get, the further away it feels.

Cave

洞

From Latin cava, from cavus 'hollow'.

The Empire State Building is Plato's Cave.

In Plato's *Republic*, Socrates describes a group of people who have lived in a cave all their lives. These people watch shadows projected on the wall and give names to these shadows. The shadows are the prisoners' reality but are not the real world. Only those who are freed from the cave will realise that the cave is a prison with dancing shadows, and these people (such as philosophers) will come to understand that the shadows on the wall are not reality at all.

To understand that the Empire State Building is unreal means you have to get out from that reality – American reality. It is like Plato's Cave. The deeper you enter into the cave, the further away you are from life itself.

The Brooklyn Eagle
布鲁克林之鹰

The *Brooklyn Eagle* was a daily newspaper published in New York City from 1841 to 1955. The building where it was produced stands by the Brooklyn Bridge and has been converted into residential apartments.

I passed an enormous brown brick-building, infinitely grand and imposing. I decided to turn back, to find out more. Standing in front of the gate, I tried to decipher an engraved plate with faint print on it. I made out that in 1846 Walt Whitman had worked here as a journalist, until he was sacked for his anti-slavery opinions.

So this is the *Brooklyn Eagle* Building. What a historic place, set right next to the thunderous long stretch of Brooklyn Bridge. The river shimmered silver blue, just as Whitman might have seen it.

On the way home, I found a bookshop and bought a copy of *Leaves of Grass*. I already had two or three Chinese translations at home. These Chinese editions have lain around in my different homes in different countries, all these years. But this was my first English copy.

Perfume

香味

From French parfum (noun), parfumer (verb), and from
outdated Italian parfumare, literally 'to smoke through'.

It was my father's generation that read Walt Whitman in Chinese. My
father and my teachers told me to look at the shapes and colours of
leaves. But I noticed leaves without having to read the book. Now I
was in America, the country of Whitman. Should I read him again?
How should I read him? Could one still find Whitman in the streets
of New York?

So, I opened the pages of *Leaves of Grass*. Suddenly, I found myself
struck by a kind of amnesia. The words before me generated none of the
feelings I associated with the Chinese edition I had read long ago. So
this is the real Whitman? And I am reading it in the real place, where
it was written. My old Whitman fell away from me. Here's a line from
the real Whitman:

> *Houses and rooms are full of perfumes . . . the shelves are crowded
> with perfumes.*

And then:

> *The atmosphere is not a perfume . . . it has no taste of the distilla-
> tion . . . it is odorless*
> *It is for my mouth forever . . . I am in love with it.*

The real Whitman is full of ellipses. I wondered about them. Were
they just the product of his mind rushing forward while his hands

struggled to keep up with getting down his impressions? Or were the gaps between his phrases part of the poetry itself? They might be a form of eloquence, as in when a sage stops speaking to allow his silence to talk. To me they seemed like the white spaces in a Chinese traditional painting, which are also part of the pictorial language.

Flipping through the book, I looked for the publication date. No, actually, the printing date. It didn't tell me. It's a Penguin edition of *Leaves of Grass*, that's it. It is a first edition. The book first appeared in 1855. He self-published it. No one was waiting to read it. It wasn't about to be stacked in the important bookshops. It was a poem to himself.

Later. After a few hours of reading Whitman, the sky was the colour of an oyster. It was raining. I forgot that in America they also have rain, just like in England. The Hudson River was still beneath me. It had not emigrated. And it was calling me. I looked at it. It was too far for me to jump in.

Harlem

哈林区

> A neighbourhood in Manhattan, New York. It was originally
> named after the city of Haarlem in the Netherlands.

I kept on sneezing violently, as I walked through the streets of Harlem.
I imagined I looked red-eyed, and viper-like. Asthma, they said, was
much more common in this area than in other parts of New York City.

A high-pitched ringing sound vibrated around the gigantic housing
project – General Grant Houses. Was it from a smoke detector, or a fire
alarm? As far as I could make out, this piercing sound had been going
on since the day I arrived in the neighbourhood. The buildings along
125th Street seemed to be perpetually drenched in it. How did people
survive in this din? Or were they so used to it that they could not hear
it any more above their own tinnitus?

There was a little statue of an angel, dim and feeble-looking, standing in a fenced yard by 128th Street. That was the place I often stopped
and pondered. I remembered reading that James Baldwin went to a
primary school in this street. But now the school was gone; only the
angel in the yard remained. I would stare at it through the fence for a
long time. There were some plastic flowers in pots around him. It was
an alien sight to me. I thought about the difference between America
and China.

Angels do not exist in China. Fairies don't need wings.

And China is very far away.

Tropical and Subtropical Moist Broadleaf Forests (TSMF)

热带亚热带湿润阔叶林

TSMF are found in large areas centred on the equatorial belt and between the tropics of Cancer and Capricorn. They are dominated by evergreen tree species. The areas include South East Asia, parts of Central Africa and the Amazon Rainforest.

I love this simple technical term: 'moist broadleaf forest'. It is exactly how I remember the vegetation in my home town – moist and broad-leaved. Not these northern trees with needle-like blades. In my southern China, the trees have palm-sized leaves. Each leaf is a small umbrella, holding a pool of raindrops. The flowers too. In my mind's eye, their mouths are always wide open, their petals thick and leathery, their ovaries stretching out stigmas and stamens to seduce insects.

And then the insects. My father once told me he saw a stick insect in Hainai Province, near the border with Vietnam. He was a landscape painter, and was on one of his life-drawing excursions.

'The strange creature looked just like a walking leaf, or a tiny ani-mated walking stick. So I put down my painting brush and touched it. Suddenly I realised it was an animal, not a dried bamboo blade!'

My father reflected, his face dreamlike as if he were still lost in a dense jungle.

That was a very long time ago. Both the broadleaved forest and my father's face are now memories. They are of the past, of a separate reality. The words I have now are traces of that past. Perhaps they will allow me to carry out an etymology of separation.

The Ramble

漫步

A Central Park woodland, known as the Ramble, composed of thirty-eight acres of winding pathways between 73rd and 78th streets. It is often noted for its birdwatching opportunities.

In Central Park, I found myself lost in a maze of woods. I had been coming to the park almost every day, but I hadn't been to this place. Where was I? The trees were tall and serene, surrounding me as if I were in some Scandinavian forest. Looking at their branches and leaves, their names slowly came into my mind. Oak, pine, cherry, hackberry. There was an impressive old tree, its spidery roots sprawling under my boots. A tag was attached to the trunk: American sycamore. Planted in 1859 during the construction of the Reservoir.

So, it is more than 150 years old, I thought. It looked to me just like an ordinary plane tree you would find in any part of London, or along

the roadside in Beijing. Though the canopy looked wider and thicker, and its bark more silver.

I wandered farther, passing over a rusty little bridge. The air smelled of hay. It was not the typical air of the city. It was quiet and peaceful here – birdsong replaced the sound of Manhattan traffic. Somewhere above my head I heard the loud cackle of woodpeckers, as I meandered through the winding paths. Walking down from a steep hillside, I was greeted by Shakespeare Garden. This mini garden was arranged with flowers and plants from Shakespeare's plays. Although it was still winter, daffodils were already blooming, along with white and pink helle-bores. Rose bushes stood inside the fence, trimmed and naked without leaves, waiting for the spring light.

So, this is the Ramble. *Ramble* is a verb, as well as a noun. I felt this word attracting me like a magnet, but I was not sure why.

I spent some hours in this urban forest. I observed a few locals' birdwatching activities. They were on a bench with their binoculars. An old man in a hat mimicked the sound of a songbird, to attract its appearance. I could only find these birdwatchers quaint. I am not very interested in birds. Still, this was a mysterious place pregnant with a range of meanings for me. Here are a few:

New Yorkers, or some of them, come here to escape the frenetic intensity of the city.

The Ramble is a labyrinth, somewhere you can get lost. In fact, it feels necessary to get lost, at least for a while. Is that how we temporarily lose ourselves?

The Ramble is similar to the centre of one's own mind, so intimate, yet unknown.

You can also ramble. As in Led Zeppelin's song 'Ramble on', one can wander out, following the need to move on.

All these facets were here at the centre of this great city. The Ramble was a place which seemed to have a different dimension. I couldn't think of any place like this in the cities I had lived in, such as London and Beijing.

Stuyvesant Town – Peter Cooper Village
斯图韦森特镇

A large residential development on the Lower East Side of Manhattan. The complex consists of 110 red-brick apartment buildings from First Avenue to Avenue C.

I was walking along First Avenue, parallel to the gigantic Stuyvesant Town–Peter Cooper Village. The concrete monster seemed to replicate itself wherever I turned. The architecture repeated, with monotonous brown and squares. I was hungry. But I didn't manage to find any interesting food stores. There was only this superblock, containing multitudes of lives unknown to me. How many floors in each building? Eighteen? Twenty? And how many people live in each tower? How many rubbish bins are offered to the residents in their backyards?

I had been walking for hours, from Midtown all the way down to the Lower East Side. My stomach was empty and I felt thirsty. Finally, I saw a bagel shop. A typical Jewish bagel shop. But behind the counter was an Asian man (Chinese or Vietnamese?). An Asian woman was counting coins. Both moved slowly and wordlessly, their eyelids half closed as if they were still asleep. They did not talk, so I could not detect their language, or accent. I rarely eat bagels. Nevertheless, I bought two with cream cheese.

Now I really wanted to get out from this concrete fortress. With my sore feet and tired legs, I wondered if I should go to Alphabet City. And from there, I could find the footpath to the Williamsburg Bridge and, eventually, arrive on the other side of the city.

Empty Space
空

The Chinese word means space, and at the same time emptiness.

I cannot find the right English word for *kong*: 空. Unoccupied? Empty? It might be *Leer* in German? *Dénué* in French? I lose my grasp of European words when I try to translate them. These words are too 'empty'. *Void* is never *kong*. It is the opposite.

The origin of the Old English 'empty' is *æmtig*, or *æmetta*, which means 'leisure'. But leisure is certainly even more remote from the Chinese idea of 空. *Kong* is both content and possibility.

My memories of men and sex are always connected to their living spaces, their apartments. When I think of 空, I often think of a young Austrian architect. It was in Vienna and we had met at a rooftop bar near the Kunst Haus, looking down on the water. It must have been the Donaukanal. I have an affinity for canals and rivers in foreign places, especially in inner cities. I feel that as long as I know the water, I will not feel too alienated there. Perhaps sleeping with someone in a foreign land is an intense way to connect to a place. To plug myself in, to be charged by a socket in a wall, to attain an elusive perspective.

The architect's apartment was furnished with nothing. It was a pristine bare space with a white bed in the middle. And that was it. There was no foreplay. The abstraction and the whiteness of the place filled me with melancholic arousal. He was gentle but forceful. It was my first and last encounter with him. His penis was youthful, and it was full in my hand. I lost track of time.

But in between embraces, I noticed a book on the floor by the bed. The cover was a black-and-white photo of a fishing hut, and the title was something to do with Wittgenstein. It was in German.

Now, years later, as I walked by the Hudson River with the sound of throbbing highway traffic in my ears, I thought of Vienna, and that Wittgenstein book on the floor. I wanted to read it. More, I wanted to know the feeling of reading it in an empty space, a space containing little but my desperate attempt to connect through a stranger's body.

Garbanzo Beans

鹰嘴豆

Often called chickpeas, both refer to a plant in the *Cicer arietinum* family. The name chickpea comes from the Latin word cicer.

I left the Hudson, and crossed Riverside Drive. I was finally in a large supermarket. I was new to the country, and did not know this part of the city – West Harlem. It leads towards Inwood, another place I had only heard of. I looked at the products I was not familiar with. I bought a can of garbanzo beans. Or should I say chickpeas? The name 'garbanzo beans' sounds exotic to a Chinese person. I remembered some lines from Allen Ginsberg's poem:

America when I was seven momma took me to Communist Cell meetings they sold us garbanzos a handful per ticket a ticket costs a nickel and the speeches were free everybody was angelic and sentimental about the workers . . .

I never understood the bit about '*they sold us garbanzos a handful per ticket*'. So, Americans would fry and then dry that sort of bean so they could sell them as snacks? In any case, it felt like a good deal for a kid attending Communist meetings. My father was a member of the local Communist Party, and when I was young he would often take me to his evening meetings. I would sit on a bench at the back of the crowded and smoky hall, with just a handful of roasted soybeans in my pocket and a stack of homework on my knees. The meetings lasted for hours, sometimes till past bedtime.

A few hours later, in my rented apartment next to the Hudson River, I opened the can and poured the beans into a boiling soup. I cleared the remaining ones from the can, and ate them. I liked the texture. Mushy but still intact, with a trustworthy earthy taste.

I thought of the Chinese name 鷹嘴豆 – the bean with an eagle's beak.

Soybeans
黄豆

The word 'soy' is thought to originate as a corruption of the Chinese names for soy sauce (Mandarin 豉油: chi you, or Cantonese: sih yàuh).

The bean with an eagle's beak.

If America is associated with garbanzo beans for a foreigner like me, then China is associated with soybeans. I think of the legumes I ate every day in my childhood. Yellow soybeans. Green edamame. Blonde broad beans. But we called all these round seeds 黄豆 – yellow beans.

My maternal grandmother's house was next to a soybean processing plant. The premises were constructed from bamboo sticks on a wooden frame, like a large hut without doors. We could enter and stand by the ever-turning mill, and watch the workmen pouring kilos of yellow beans into the grinder. We could also enter the cooking place where they processed the blended bean curd into tofu. It was not really a kitchen, there were no woks or pots, just a large brick platform built on the ground with a fire underneath. When the fire was not burning, the tofu makers, mainly men, who were barefoot, would step onto the cooking platform and stamp on the bean curd to flatten the solid mass. I always worried about whether the men had washed their feet before trampling all over the pale yellow blobs. But their feet were as white and as pale as the beans, even though their arms and faces were deeply tanned. And they were always covered in sweat. Their sweat rolled down from their cheeks, like syrupy beans, dripping onto the steamed mash.

'Such hard work, as hard as growing rice in the paddies!' My parents would say this to me while buying a kilo of freshly made tofu, still steaming and hot.

Sometimes, my brother and I would also go to the processing plant to buy freshly brewed soy sauce, collecting it in two large tin cans. We would then walk out, passing donkeys arriving loaded with supplies of fresh beans in baskets. We would go home sauntering along the river which passed by my grandmother's house. I remember the large pebble stones on the riverbed and how clear the water was. I could see shrimp and eels swimming in the stream. In the near distance, I could see fields of rapeseed flowers and tea plantations on the hills, which had been tended by the locals for centuries. But before long, I was separated from that familiar landscape – the semi-tropical climate, the vegetation, the mountainous surroundings, the agricultural life. Not only from that landscape, but also from direct contact with the earth itself – crops growing in the spring and maturing in the autumn and then being metamorphosed through food processing. My separation from that kind of life has been absolute. I have not returned to that part of the world for many years.

Dwell

栖

The word is of Germanic origin. It is related to Middle
Dutch dwellen.

I was reading in my room while dusk descended on the Hudson. I
could not concentrate, because I was frustrated that I was too late that
afternoon to register for health care in a downtown office. It was Friday.
I still did not have my Social Security number. Without it I could not
get paid or open a bank account in the United States.

I ruminated on the concept of dwelling – 栖. Can I relocate myself
again, having already moved to a new continent once? 'To dwell' is
different from 'to live'. To dwell is to settle in a particular place. The
Chinese character 栖 comes with the 'tree' radical 木. To settle down
is to live beside trees, among woods. If there are no trees, there is
no home. One of the earliest quotes about the concept of living is
from the philosopher Zhuangzi, 2,400 years ago: 居处也,处心至一
之道. Zhuangzi explains that home is a place to inhabit where the
heart can settle, and that it is a way towards *Tao* – the natural flow
of all things.

Dwell. This is a Germanic word. Perhaps the most famous usage of
this word is in German poet Friedrich Hölderlin's poem, 'In lieblicher
Bläue' (In Lovely Blue):

> *Is God unknown? Does he manifest as the sky?*
> *This I tend to believe. It is the measure of the man.*
> *Well deserving, yet poetically we dwell on this earth.*

We are supposed to dwell on this earth poetically. Martin Heidegger used this concept in one of his most well-known essays, 'Poetically, Man Dwells'. He believed we dwell altogether unpoetically in this world, but the inner poetry is always there. I'm not sure, but I want to agree. Life is a vast spiderweb of trivial tasks. Renting a flat and dealing with energy bills and the cost of living; finding an accountant and seeing a dentist without fearing the bills; eating, cleaning, excreting. We live in a confined urban space with a few pot plants on the windowsills under light bulbs. Yet there is poetry to be uncovered, or at least I like to think so. Sometimes I feel dwelling and poetry belong to each other, only because there is inner poetry in our yearning for this connection. Though sometimes I wonder if life has no meaning at all. We try to make meaning because we cannot bear there being none.

The light was fading, I wanted to get ready for bed. When one is alone, one sleeps either very early or very late. Maybe the strange New York sirens would wake me. The sirens in America have different sounds to those in Europe. They wail with short but constant splatterings, like a demented whale weeping.

Hudson River

哈德逊河

A river that flows from north to south through eastern
New York.

There was the constant drone of sirens along the riverbank that night.
They did wake me up. Perhaps I went to sleep too early. I got up.
I switched on the light. It was only ten in the evening. It was too
early to go back to sleep in any case. I got dressed, took my keys
and went out.

Like a sleepwalker, I wandered without direction. I was aware that
there were no stars at all in this part of New York. Even the Hudson
River was completely illuminated by both sides of the cityscape. New
Jersey was out there, with millions of lit buildings, as awake as Manhattan. I walked down the slope of the riverbank. Suddenly I noticed
my shoes were wet, and one foot was on a rock submerged in the water.
I could see almost everything on the fluid surface. I could see algae,
some little drifters, a Coke can stuck in between floating branches. I
bent down, and half sat on a branch which spread out behind me. I saw
something moving in the wet sand. A little creature. I brought my face
closer. I could not see what it was. An airplane passed above me. Then
another. I looked up. Were they coming or going? I looked down into
the sand again. This time, I saw a little crab, digging in and out beside
my feet. A crab – grey, modest and discreet.

I watched the movement of the little crab for a long time, until it disappeared. I saw myself as this crawling thing. I did. I imagined myself

moulting, trying to come out from my old skin, hiding away until the new shell hardened. It must be a hard business.

Moulting

蜕皮

An animal sheds its old skin or feathers in order to grow.

I waited for a while by the Hudson River, to see if I would find the crab again, or some other little creatures. But I only saw the quiet shimmering water under the illuminated Manhattan sky. The night was growing more peaceful. It must have been past midnight by now. I decided to return to my apartment.

I went back to bed and read about crabs' moulting. When a crab moults, the old shell softens and erodes away, while a new shell forms. At the time of shedding, the creature takes in a lot of water so that it will expand and can crack open the old shell. The creature must then extract all of itself, including its legs, the lining of the digestive tract, its mouthparts and eyestalks. This is a difficult process that takes many hours, and if a crab gets stuck, it will die. I could not help trying to imagine the two eyestalks being prised out of their encasements! And if the crab fails to bring out its eyes, would the creature survive as an eyeless animal? After this process, the crab is finally free from its own bony prison but it is extremely soft, and it must hide until its new shell has hardened.

So the little thing I saw in the shallows of the Hudson River could have been hiding away after moulting. Or perhaps it was looking for a rock under which to shed its shell, but my appearance had disturbed it. Or might it have been on its way to mate? Apparently, mating happens just after a female crab has shed its old skin.

The home of a crab is its own shell. It lives in that home for a while then abandons it, and creates a new one. That's not unlike us humans. Our house is the exterior of our bodies, and we can move out or abandon it, and then make a new house. But some people get stuck in their particular lives and are unable to come out. Just like some crabs, they die in their old skins unable to fully moult.

The heating was too high. I opened my windows, and stood there for a while watching the sky and the river below. While the chilly wind blew my hair, a tumble of thoughts flew about like troublesome insects. I thought of the fact that I was in the US by myself, having left my child and her father in England. What was I doing, pacing around at midnight in this foreign city? Perhaps I was searching for adventures and encounters and, ultimately, some sort of freedom that I had never had in China or Britain. But what was this freedom? Illusion, delusion or unrealised possibility? Or was it the freedom beyond a woman's house, with or without a room of her own? My thoughts were insubstantial and weightless. The night river was real and so were the lights of New Jersey on the other side. Was there freedom in this city?

I thought of women's freedom. Then I thought of children, family, possessions. I thought of the physicality of female bodies and the judgements of society. To find freedom, you have to be able to describe yourself and where you are in your life. I knew that a vocabulary fit to describe the limits of women's freedom had already been forged by generations of feminists, and by contemporary social media. But this is a generalised vocabulary for all women, whether white or black, whether working or unemployed, whether married or single. In this, I could not find a lexicon for myself. Each woman needs to find her own words, that private, special vocabulary she can use to express her condition. To make these words her own she needs to embark upon an etymological journey deep within herself. The words that will be in her possession can be shared, but not turned into slogans. They cannot be taken away from the particular. In that sense I am neither woman nor Asian, neither worker nor oppressed citizen. I am just a human who cannot overcome, or deny, a very specific past, set in stone, real, unfathomably rich in detail, loaded with a finely wrought mesh of social baggage.

I had been enveloped in a sense of my own troubled reality since I arrived here. I felt threatened by the real possibility of a deep and irrevocable separation from my past, and by being in between worlds. I was experiencing a dreadful sense of incompleteness. A thick melancholy like the night fog upon the Hudson lay on me. If a crab had its own private language, fit to describe its own sentient history, then what is my lexicon, which describes this being that I am? I, this person looking out at the dark river now, had these feelings that couldn't be caught in a net of ready-made words, nor paved over by any familiar lexicon. If we are honest, we must acknowledge our deep need to communicate, beyond the rigid vocabulary of feminism and politics, and to reach for a language that is authentic yet remains uncategorised. We are trying to articulate something, but it's intangible. I looked outside trying to find the moon or the stars, but none were visible, in the drenching light of New York City.

2

Radical: 女

(female, girl, woman)

Woman
女

Old English: wīfmon, -man; Middle English: wif, wiif, wyf.

A Chinese character can be composed of a number of radicals, or just one single radical. For example, the radical for female or woman is 女 – *nu*. But 女 is also a complete and independent character.

If one practises calligraphy with a paintbrush, the image of a woman appears more figurative than the computer-generated character.

甲骨文　　　金文　　　小篆　　　楷体

The above characters are all *nu* – woman. They show the changes from ancient times to modern day. The first image is from the oracle bone script, carved on turtle shell. The second is bronzeware script, from around 3,000 years ago. The third image is standardised seal script from the Qin Dynasty 2,000 years ago. And the last image is the current simplified standard *hanzi*.

The older images look much more like this: a woman is a person on her knees. Why is she kneeling? Does she kneel down to pray to the sky, to her god? Or to her ancestors? To her father? Her husband? To the chief of her tribe? Or maybe she is literally bowing before her master's penis?

One can change or remove this feudal and traditional radical from a dictionary, but one cannot eradicate this concept from our past. Because that image, that symbol, has recorded *our* very history, a female one and a male one. A human history. A history of oppression and exploitation. It's one of the narratives of *Homo sapiens*.

We can change a word, an image, but we cannot overwrite history.

Man / Human
人 / 男人

Sanskrit: manu – mankind. Old English: mann,
Proto-Germanic origin.

The Chinese character for human is 人 (ren). An upright thing with
two legs. The Chinese character is both female and male; it is gender
neutral. In the West, the generic term *man* has historically been used
to include women, but it is not gender neutral. It is masculine.

In China, we don't usually speak 'as a man', or 'as a woman', we
always speak 'as a ren' (作为一个人), or 'my humble self' (本人).
My father's generation would say only 'my humble self'. When I was
growing up I regarded myself as a punk and I did not speak like that.
I referred to myself as '人一 ren'. But since I came to the West, I find
myself speaking like this: 'as a woman, I feel . . .'. I have the sense that
this phrase tries to define me, or confine me, to put me into a certain
place with closed doors. And now it reminds me of my current reality:
my child who is not with me, my constructed home back in England,
and all that domesticity I am trying to escape.

Today I was in the Harlem Library. It was bitterly cold outside, with
a high wind. Inside there was a strange smell, musty and stained, not
from the old books, but perhaps from the carpet or from the people
sitting around me. Sweaters, trousers, coats, eyes gazing down to the
pages. The forecast said the Arctic blast was on its way and it would
snow tonight. I would like to see this city after snowfall.

Übermensch

超人，神人

German, translated as 'overman', 'superman'. German root: über 'over'.

'I teach you the overman. Man is something that shall be overcome. What have you done to overcome him?' (*Thus Spoke Zarathustra*, Nietzsche)

In Chinese, 超人 – superhuman – is a translated concept from Western literature.

The snow did fall during the night, and I kept the heating on. It was a quiet night. I read until I fell asleep. A philosophy book. Not typical bedtime reading perhaps. But my choice was in part due to J, the father of my child in London. J is a philosopher. He teaches Nietzsche's work. He often talks to me about Nietzsche, and Nietzsche's friendship with the composer Wagner. It was odd that I began to read Nietzsche in America. I could have read more relevant books, Steinbeck or Hemingway, something rooted here.

Still, there I was, trying to read *Thus Spoke Zarathustra* with the snow falling soundlessly outside. Then the night mood entered my body and I fell asleep. The image of the philosopher stayed in my dreams. A strange hard-headed man with a moustache. J came into my dream too. He was speaking German, not very well I suspected, though I did not understand his words.

The image of Zarathustra also lingered. In the book, Zarathustra comes down from the mountain to the real world. He enters a town and walks around a marketplace in his ragged robe. Among sellers and buyers, he tells everyone that God is dead. He speaks these words out loud:

> *Behold, I teach you the overman! The overman is the meaning of the earth. Let your will say: the overman shall be the meaning of the earth! I beseech you, my brothers, remain faithful to the earth, and do not believe those who speak to you of otherworldly hopes!*

Übermensch – the overman. I guessed what Nietzsche intended was for man to abandon the Christian God and to assume full responsibility to create his own values. Somehow the concept felt very masculine for me. Is there an über-woman? Every month when I see my menstrual blood, and recall the bodily ordeal of childbirth, I find no over-woman. It's more like an under-woman. Woman is equal to the bleeding of the body, the open wound, and the weight of the earth. Still, Nietzsche was himself a semi-invalid, a man suffering all sorts of physical afflictions. He wrote about bodily pains, disappointment and loneliness. So perhaps his *Übermensch* is more a Buddhistic idea. It's about embracing life, even all its deficiencies and suffering.

I used to talk to J about this. But now I was in the US, and our conversations had stopped.

In the morning, I woke up in the dry heat. I did not see the blanket of white I had hoped would be covering Riverside Park and the streets of Harlem. It was wet and grey, with some snow-dust here and there on the distant roofs.

The A Train
地铁A线

A train line on the New York City Subway.

I remember almost every detail of my first meeting with E. I remember that I could not find the restaurant and was late, and how I finally entered the place, weary and apologetic.

It was a very windy day, my hair was a mess. I wore a grey wool sweater that did not belong to me. I had found it back in London, in my apartment after a dinner party. Someone had left it on a chair and had never claimed it. It had a manly style and it was warm, the only warm clothing I had brought with me to New York. How absurd, I thought, it was the ugliest sweater I ever wore but I had chosen it for this meeting with E.

The restaurant was on Broadway, obscured by scaffolding. I judged the atmosphere of the place in order to get a sense of E. Before then we had communicated only by email. E was polite and restrained. His sombre expression drew me to him. The food on the menu was not inspiring. Fries and omelette, otherwise some suspiciously sourced meat. Filter coffee served in a big pot. E looked at me leafing through the menu, and remarked:

'Perhaps you can't find anything to eat on this menu.'

It was a humorous comment, for my ears, and I thought he was observant and sensitive. Or was I too obvious? My expression, my transparent manner, my foreigner's behaviour, all manifested in a certain uneasiness in front of him. And E was a semi-local who had lived in this part of town for the last thirty years. During lunch I talked non-stop, to cover my uneasiness. I spoke about my writing and teaching; I talked briefly about my past in China and in Britain. E told me about his work. I did not ask where he originally came from. Mainly he listened to me.

Then E paid the bill. We came out, and lingered in front of the restaurant. He would head back to the north, along Riverside Park, while I had to go south. I asked him where I could catch the A train.

The A train? E repeated, and seemed to be perplexed. I don't know about the A Train, I only ever take the Number 1 train downtown. He added: I am very provincial.

Provincial. I was surprised by what E said. Someone like E cannot be provincial. He had lived in different continents like me. We had both lived multiple lives in multiple languages. Perhaps only someone who had lived such a life would dare to claim to be provincial.

We went our separate ways. I descended into the subway. I did not find the A train. The next train came and carried me off. Even today, I don't remember why I needed the A train. Was it because of Duke Ellington's song 'Take the A Train'? To get to Harlem you have to take the A Train, the song says. I associated the part of Manhattan where I was staying with that piece of music.

Mother

妈

Old English – mōdor, Dutch – moeder, German – Mutter; from
an Indo-European root shared by Latin – mater, Greek – mētēr.

Remember how the radical for woman looks? It is 女 – a woman kneeling down, as if she is praying. Now I think of the character 妈 – mother.

'Mother' in Chinese is composed of two signs. The radical for
woman: 女, and the radical for horse: 马. Woman plus horse is mother.
There is no direct connection between horse and mother. The horse
(ma) serves a phonetic function, to help to pronounce the combined
character.

I often think of my mother. The images I have of her are not happy
ones. I see her worried face, perpetually frowning; the thinning hair
on the top of her head; her heavy body moving about in the kitchen;
her short legs struggling on our staircase. She was a woman who never
enjoyed life. Human life for her was all about suffering and endurance.
My mother hardly ever cried, but I remember seeing her weeping once.
She was in her bedroom; her foot had been injured in an accident. I
thought that her tears were to do with the injury. But now I think of
it, I realise her grief was about her husband, who was rarely home. My
father had always travelled, ever since I was young. I remember my
mother wiping away her tears, walking into the kitchen and starting to
cook, as if nothing had happened. I also remember my mother being
cruel to my paternal grandmother. Jealousy around one man, my father.
The two women could not live under one roof. One was born under
Feudalism, the other under Communism. Now the two women, my

mother and my grandmother, are both gone. Their ashes have been scattered in the wind, along with their suffering. But the images of them kneeling and praying have stayed with me, just like the radical for women: 女.

Infatuation
痴情

From Latin fatuus 'foolish', infatuat- 'made foolish', from the
verb infatuare.

But in America, I didn't think of my mother or my grandmother so
much. My mind was occupied by my experiences of new encounters
here, with people, and with a new landscape.

My memories of the early days with E are associated with the bars
we went to, the drinks we ordered, and those little taverns around Harlem. But his physical presence in public spaces was very different from
the private one. In E's apartment, he was relaxed, and his long arms and
legs seemed to open towards me, through the constraint of his clothes.

A kiss was in the air, waiting for the moment our lips would come
together. We anticipated that togetherness when I entered the apartment. Or was it even before I came to his place?

There were two couches in E's living room. I chose to sit on the less
imposing one. Perhaps the large sofa suggested something obvious for
me – would we lie down on it together? On that smaller couch, he sat
beside me. I don't remember if we had drinks or not. We must have
had some, our affair had always involved alcohol. We often drank from
evening till midnight, in bars and at home, clothed, naked, as long as
we were together.

The first time, at some point, the zip on my dress was unfastened, by
my own hand, and then by his. It slipped onto the floor. Then the bra.
It must have been me – my hands unhooking them. I was impatient,
and aching for him.

He touched my nipples. His caress was reserved, even remote.

No, we didn't go on from there. We didn't. His tongue was shy, and mine too. They were afraid, and hidden behind our thoughts. We kissed, but we were still outside our skin, held back by this strangeness between us.

Tribeca

翠贝卡

A neighbourhood in New York City, its name is a syllabic abbreviation of 'Triangle Below Canal Street'.

I first witnessed American cops arresting black people in Tribeca. I might have walked past a shooting that afternoon without realising it. I thought I had heard a gunshot but did not conclude that it was a shooting. My idea of gunfire is what you get in movies and theatres, not in the real world. Later that day in Tribeca, I walked into a confusion of policemen and cars between Greenwich Street and Franklin Street. I was told there had been a shooting. And not far from me, I could see two black men with guns pressed on their backs lined up against a police vehicle, arms behind their heads. There were shouts, struggles and handcuffings. I looked at the weapons attached to the hip of a police officer near me. He had a taser. It looked like a kid's ray gun. He also had a pistol, or was that a revolver? Then all of sudden, I was ushered away by someone, redirecting me to an exit where I could see the river.

The only time I have touched a real gun was almost thirty years ago. It was during the first months of my university years in Beijing, as part of my military education. We were in a camp of a branch of the People's Liberation Army, far away from the city centre. We were all eighteen or nineteen years old, away from home for the first time, leading a collective dormitory life. After three months of training, and practising with dummy guns under supervision, in the final week we were given real rifles – long, heavy, dark and metallic – to shoot targets. It was a nerve-racking day. I cannot remember the moment my fingers pressed the trigger of the heavy rifle in my hands. Nor the smell or the kick as it fired. All I remember was that after shooting it, we were told to find our mark on the target. Since I have bad eyesight, I had to walk all the way to the distant bullseye to see the result. And as I stood in front of the ringed board, there came a shout from behind me: Girl! You hit nothing but the sky! What a waste!

But right now, I was stuck in Lower Manhattan, and I needed to get out from the police-infested Tribeca. As I finally managed to escape the controlled streets, I heard a song playing loudly, coming out from one of the windows above my head. It was 'Empire State of Mind' by Alicia Keys and Jay-Z. After the rapping, the great and ever familiar lines rocketed into the sky, and descended on the river. Their voices reverberated: 'In New York'. Then came a resounding 'concrete jungle'. Of course, this is where dreams are made, or broken.

Faun

法翁

From Roman mythology: a lustful rural god, half-man half-goat.

Before I visited E's apartment again, I spent my afternoons in Morningside Park. I would follow the path alongside the Cathedral of St John the Divine and walk down the hill. The cathedral has a beautiful bushy courtyard. One afternoon I saw a small white peacock, quietly strolling in front of a side door of the building. I was mesmerised. Such an unusual sight in urban New York. Was it semi-wild, or domesticated? Why did it not walk away and escape? Of course there was nowhere to go, just the busy traffic of Amsterdam Avenue nearby. If it was kept by the cathedral, was it just for the purpose of entertainment? No one was around, no eager tourist taking photos. I stared at the strolling peacock for a while. Was it a sign? Ominous or lucky? I thought of my grandmother, who saw a white peacock before marrying my grandfather. It proved to be a sorrowful marriage. That was a very long time ago. Should I believe something might happen to me soon, in this city, at this stage of my life? The peacock looked back at me idly, without giving a sign. I took a photo of it and left the yard. I went down the steps leading to Morningside Park.

There were never many people in this park. Some parts of it were almost eerily empty. At the time I didn't know it was dangerous, nor did I know that recently a girl from Barnard College had been robbed and murdered while walking up the same steps I was descending. No, I was not aware of any of that. Each time I came to this park, my intention was to spend some time by my Chinese pond. Of course it is not called the

Chinese pond; it is an artificial pond with cliffs and rocks and a fountain, overhung by a weeping willow. But it looked perfectly Chinese to me. Even the willow tree with its soft bending branches touching the mossy water resembled the willows in my Chinese home town. I liked standing by the pond or sitting by it, looking at the water and the dramatic cliff. The fountain was the only object that was non-Chinese to me. Known as the Seligman Fountain (Bear and Faun), it has a rather complex design: a dark-hued cave, on top of which lies a bear looking down on a faun. A bear and a faun! It seemed to me a strange combination, something from the Western imagination.

It struck me that the word *faun* as well as its image has no Chinese equivalent. A lustful god, half-man half-goat, is surely not a very Buddhist imagining. So there I was, staring at the little faun, not long after seeing a peacock in the afternoon light.

I never told E about the peacock. I don't know why I didn't. Perhaps I worried that the bird might be an inauspicious sign. But the faun with goat's legs? Yes, that seemed to be fine to me. Surely there was something lustful going on, in my mind, and perhaps in his mind too.

Amerindian

亚马逊人，美洲印第安人

Adjective and noun, blend of American and Indian.

That first morning together, after E woke up and saw me cutting apples in his kitchen for breakfast, he said:

'You have such beautiful skin. Is it because you eat so much fruit and vegetables? Sometimes you look Amerindian, as well as everything else. All the beauty of the world in a face.'

I wasn't sure about the beauty of the world in a face, but I thought about a female Amerindian. I stepped back from myself and tried to understand how I might look like an Amerindian to him: a black-haired brown-skinned woman speaking broken English, who is often confused by the circumstances around her.

One can never see oneself clearly. We are all our own Empire State Buildings. After all this time, I wondered, could I see myself with more clarity in America? I had just come out of a cave, after years of playing with dancing shadows on the wall. Would I enter another one? A new one with American stories playing out on the screen?

Lebenskünstler / Lebenskünstlerin
生活艺术家

German, a life artist, someone who lives their life as an artwork.

E taught translation at a university, specialising in European languages. He also understood animal language, and was an expert on Beethoven. Since I knew little about Beethoven, and nothing about animal language, I admired E. I wanted to possess E in order to possess his knowledge.

'I have nothing to hang on to, not even my family in London,' I once said to him, feeling unmotivated and uprooted. 'The only refuge is creative work – making art.'

E knew of my melancholy, and he responded: 'Yes, that's what Beethoven believes. Only art.'

But Beethoven, in my opinion, hardly had any *life* in an ordinary sense. Genius was his sole possession, otherwise he was angry and intolerant for most of his life. Since God decided that the man didn't deserve ordinary love or domestic comfort, it was obvious that he would have to seek refuge in art.

'You quote Beethoven, but I'll quote Oscar Wilde,' I responded. 'Wilde said, "I put my talent in my art but I use my genius in my life."'

'You are a *Lebenskünstler* then.'

'You mean *Lebenskünstlerin*, female noun.'

'Yes. You are a *Lebenskünstlerin*, a woman who manages to deal with problems of life in an artful way. A master of living, an artist of life.'

Who might be a *Lebenskünstler*? Or a *Lebenskünstlerin*? Walt Whitman? Colette? Marcel Duchamp? Neal Cassady? Or none of them. Not a working artist whose sole purpose in life is to create art. A gardener has a greater chance of being a *Lebenskünstler* than an artist. It is difficult to conceive that a good writer could be a *Lebenskünstlerin*. If someone has a way to transform life into art, why would they need to devote their life to something else, rather than to life itself?

A sage or a stoic philosopher deals with life and finds peace, without making his life an artwork. In fact, he or she doesn't need to escape into art, but accepts life as it is. Is this actually a less illusion-prone way of being? I wondered about all this, and did not continue our discussion. But I continued to be drawn to the idea of a *Lebenskünstlerin*.

Femmes Fatale / Man-eater / Vamp
致命女郎 / 狐狸精

Reference in Eastern culture: Daji, 妲己, the favourite consort of
the last king of the Shang Dynasty in China 3,000 years ago. She
is portrayed as a malevolent fox spirit, and considered a classic
example of how a beautiful woman can cause the downfall of a
dynasty.

There is a large sports complex in Riverside State Park. It was built on
top of a sewage treatment facility. While walking around the area, I
could smell the faint odour of the sewage. Still, there is a nice swimming
pool inside and I contemplated getting membership. But it depended
on how long I was going to stay in America. E said I should sign up,
and he would get me a swimsuit too.

One evening we went there and were about to buy the swimsuit. In the middle of a conversation, E suddenly admitted that he was afraid of me. He feared that I would take away everything from him – his life, his work, his independence. I was taken aback. I felt hurt.

For a while, I was unable to say anything about my feelings. Some days later, I asked him if he thought I was a female fatale. He responded, no, not really. I assumed that he wanted to sound relaxed, or maybe he had forgotten his fear temporarily.

I thought of *The Magic Flute* – the opera I saw once. Each time the Queen of the Night appeared on the stage, her wonderful costume (her crown, her enormous winged dress) and the lighting around her created such a powerfully dramatic effect. Her sheer presence induces fear in everyone around her. She either demands the impossible or takes away what belongs to her people. But I was not that sort of queen, nor did I feel I had any power over E. I was driven simply by lust.

We bought a black one-piece bathing suit. But I never wore it, as I never went back to the sports centre to swim. Each time I passed the park I gazed at the swimming-pool building. For some reason, we never set foot in the place again.

Crossing Brooklyn Ferry
布鲁克林渡船

Title of a poem by Walt Whitman, written in 1856 in
New York City.

We were crossing the Brooklyn Bridge, looking down at the water
beneath. It was not so much a crossing, actually, we just wanted to
walk above the East River, to be together in the space in between, and
had no intention of descending on the Brooklyn side at all. That day we
did not need to go to Brooklyn, or return to Manhattan, for that matter.
We wanted to hang out, hang about, between the two sides, along the
bridge's impressive span.

I saw a ferry going towards Brooklyn, its bottom black, and upper
deck white and blue. I could see myself sitting on that ferry, but not
waving like some people were doing to us at that moment. I thought
of Whitman again. 'Crossing Brooklyn Ferry' is one of my favourite
poems. The poet wrote to future New Yorkers:

> *I am with you, you men and women of a generation, or ever so many*
> *generations hence,*
>> *Just as you feel when you look on the river and the sky, so I felt . . .*
>> *I too lived, Brooklyn of ample hills was mine,*
>> *I too walk'd the streets of Manhattan Island . . .*

As I looked down at the water, I felt the poet's spirit, so quintes-
sentially American. And of course, Whitman *is* America, the same
America that built its Empire State Building. This was almost automatic: I thought of Whitman as America as I thought of Dickens as

England. It's coherent. But this sort of association never works when I think of China in relation to its writers. Because I know China so well, and for me China is never a single thing. I have to immediately separate China into different times and symbols. The ancient China with Taoist monks and untouched landscapes, imperial China with its mandarins, merchants and poets, pre-Mao China ravaged by wars and ideologies, Communist China flooded with Red Guards and factory workers on bikes, and the postmodern China that came after my departure from the country.

That day, while walking on the Brooklyn Bridge, E reminded me that the water is salty. Yes, we were very close to the ocean, even though the river is tamed within its straight banks with multitudes of skyscrapers on both sides. The moon pulls, the tide fluctuates. But right then and there, I did not understand the tides of the East River. The traffic under the bridge's footpath throbbed and echoed. So loud, no one could speak at a normal volume, or hear each other. A slight vertigo gripped me. That was the force of New York City. What would Whitman sing about this sound, this 'perfume' of the diesels, and this body electric of the masses?

Flâneur / Flâneuse
步行者

French, an idler, a man who saunters around the streets of a city.

It is awful to realise that almost all the great walkers of literature are men – Charles Baudelaire, Walter Benjamin, Robert Walser, Oscar Wilde, all flâneurs. No flâneuse. In Baudelaire's Paris or Benjamin's Berlin, a female flâneur was a prostitute: a streetwalker.

Obviously, women must have wanted to wander and to record their wanderings in written form. The absence of 'flâneuse' in literature reflects the reality that women's freedom has been and still is limited, and that if a woman wanders alone at night or even in broad daylight she might be molested or raped. It still happens everywhere in the world – in the countryside, in cities, and even in front of one's own house.

Of course, I have walked through the villages and cities in which I have lived. In my aimless walks, especially when I was young, I met plenty of molesters. A country road to school, or a quiet corner by the village market. And we know that most women admit as much. But on those paths, whether crowded or desolate, whether rainy or snowy, I have felt an unstoppable desire which drives me along, in those open spaces.

I enjoy walking for its accidental encounters, its novelty. I don't do it because I want to prove something grand, like a man documenting his month-long walk from Berlin to Istanbul, or from the east coast of America to the west coast. But as a woman walking alone, I don't always feel at ease talking to strangers. When I pass a man on an empty street,

I'm subjected to his gaze and his remarks. Men feel that they own public spaces. Women are trespassers in their domain. We are fair game.

When I walk in the West I sometimes think of walking in China. The atmosphere in the streets is very different. Generally, I feel safer in China, partly because I know the culture well, partly because the rigid Communist system has created a more controlled public space. My walks there are often wondrous experiences, especially in the remote countryside. A solitary walk can be punctuated by chance meetings and events. Once, on a village road, I met a funeral parade with wailing mourners carrying a coffin, headed by a marching band. And shortly after that I encountered a joyful wedding scene by the same dirt road, with banquet tables, drinking guests, and fireworks exploding above the revellers' heads. Warm rough hands dragged me into the celebrations and offered me a seat before mountains of dumplings and steamed buns.

I think of my grandmother. She walked very slowly, because of her bound feet. Once, she had to cross mountains and farmlands with her father to get to a village where her future husband lived. That was the only long walk she took in her entire life. Of course, that was another time, and another kind of walk. For a woman of her class and time, being a flâneuse would have been a suspicious luxury. After all, it is a literary concept created by Western bohemians in urban societies.

X

'X is a letter, which, though found in Saxon words, begins
no word in the English language.' (*A Dictionary of English
Language*, Samuel Johnson)

My name starts with X, but only in the Western version of my Chinese
name.

No word in the English language starts with X. This, at least, is what
Samuel Johnson believed. Or to be more precise, he had in mind that
no word in Latin begins with the letter X: it is always preceded by a
vowel, as in *rex* (king), or *lex* (law). Johnson was a curious man. Why
did he hold this curious view?

The term X is used in mathemat-
ics for an unknown quantity. X can
be variable. It can take any range of
values, so it's inherently suspicious
and shifty. The term X-ray also holds
this sense of X, for unknowns yet to
be discovered. This makes me think
of the famous painting by American
artist John Singer Sargent: *The Portrait of Madame X*.

White flesh in a black satin dress,
with her face turning away. Madame
X looks unknown, perhaps unknow-
able, a woman with a hidden history

radiating from her pale skin, and from her averted face. Had he been around, Dr Johnson, a man of concrete particularity, might have found all this indeterminacy disturbing. No wonder he did not want X in his English.

Xenon starts with X, and is now a proper English word, according to the *OED*. Originally, the word is from late-nineteenth-century Greek. *Xenon* is the neuter of *xenos*. It means *strange*.

Foreign / Xenos
异族

In Latin, foris and foras, meaning 'outsider'. And fores is 'door'.
In German, Ausländer. In Chinese, 异族 means 'a different tribe'.

At the beginning of the Covid-19 pandemic, President Trump claimed that the virus was a 'foreign virus', having revised his earlier description, the 'Chinese virus'.

Foreign is a powerful word. It is an essential word as long as the nation state exists, and identity politics permeate every corner of our lives.

The word *foreign* makes me think of the word *hospitality*. One of the most well known of Confucius's sayings is:

有朋自远方来, 不亦乐乎?
Isn't it joyful, when a visitor comes from afar?

One might laugh at the naivety of such a statement. But it demonstrates that in most traditional cultures, hospitality is a key virtue, and that strangers and visitors are not threatening forces. A stranger or a visitor might be a foreigner, a xenon. This foreigner would most probably speak a different language, and have different customs. We are all clothed by culture and language, and to be caught clothed in a different way is the predicament of the foreigner.

I have been a foreigner since I was twenty-nine, when I left Beijing for Europe. Being a foreigner is part of who I am. I was in some ways at home in Britain, and now I was trying to build something similar in the USA. But part of me is always in exile. We may think we are integrating and have taken in the local ways, after years of living in a new land. But then we can be rudely awakened out of the illusion of having lost our foreignness. For example, if you don't understand the local humour, you are not a local even if you have lived in the same place for a decade or more. I once went to a stand-up comedy show in London with an English friend, sitting near the front of the stage in a packed theatre. The performer delivered gag after gag, and stories with animated gestures. A steady stream of laughter surrounded me but I wasn't laughing at all. I was the only one in the room not laughing, in fact. I understood most of the words the comedian used, but I did not get any of his jokes. I felt very alien. I also felt insulted by this strong sense of smug, insider knowledge – I was not let into the gang. I must have looked like some humourless oddball, or an anthropologist from Mars. But I decided to sit through it, even though it was painful, hoping that my foreignness could be washed out in the native sea.

Immigration
迁居移民

From the Latin verb immigrare, in- 'into' + migrare 'migrate'.

Apparently, Noah Webster, author of *An American Dictionary of the English Language*, published in 1828, invented the word 'immigration'. This is probably not quite accurate. Webster took from variations of the word 'migrate', including 'commigrate', 'transmigrate', 'emigrate' and 'remigrate', to create an entry for 'immigration'.

This is Webster's 1806 definition of 'to immigrate': 'to remove into a country'. It's similar to 'emigrate': 'to remove from place to place'. Here is the Webster dictionary's more refined 1928 definition of 'to immigrate': 'to remove into a country for the purpose of permanent residence'.

When Noah Webster died in 1843, Ellis Island in New York was not yet an immigration port. It was a military base. Only a few years later, the government decided that it would serve as a processing station for new arrivals. Within ten years, the island had dealt with almost 10 million people 'removing into the country'. By 1883, the reputation of the USA as a beacon for immigrants had grown. Emma Lazarus published her sonnet about 'the huddled masses', 'The New Colossus', the new colossus being the Statue of Liberty. The land of the free was a land of immigrants. It's interesting that Noah Webster, a radical nationalist, invented such a word before the idea of immigration became part of the reinvention of the USA's sense of identity.

I have never been to Ellis Island; the closest I have come is Governor's Island in the bay between New York and New Jersey. Standing on a rock from Picnic Point, I could see the statue and an island vaguely in the distance. The copper-green body with its raised torch was like a numinous being in the mist, but at the same time kitsch, like a super-hero from a famous cartoon.

Unrequited Love
单相思

This is falling in love with someone who does not return your love, precious though it is. The Chinese word, 单相思, literally means 'single person's nostalgia'.

Shortly after E and I met, I thought of these words – unrequited love – while I was walking up and down Harlem. My heart was in self-confinement, and my pride stopped me from reaching out to E. I did not want to behave too directly, especially having had some experience with different forms of love, as well as with J and our child still in England.

The expression 'unrequited love' feels old-fashioned to me, like a concept from the days when courtly love or romantic melancholy was a virtue. Goethe has his sorrowful Werther, who ended up committing suicide. Eugene Onegin wandered the streets of St Petersburg, forlorn and abandoned, drinking too much vodka. But since I had been reading Nietzsche recently, and had been writing to J about it, I thought of Nietzsche's love life. I thought about his tortured friendship with Lou Andreas-Salomé. Lou was a young and brilliant woman, a Russian émigré, who later became a Freudian psychoanalyst in Germany. She met Nietzsche through his friend, Paul Rée. The three travelled together through Switzerland trying to live an unconventional friendship, a marriage of minds. But Nietzsche, very traditionally, wanted to marry Lou. She had no interest in that; she was so much more radical than he was in this respect. She repelled his advances which caused the philosopher distress for a period of his life. As they moved on,

Nietzsche considered his unrequited love to be the root cause of a lack of intimacy throughout his life.

I know it's strange that figures like these come into my mind when I think about my own relationships. But they do. The most important thing in my life now is the life of the mind, and my writing is the major part of it. I thought, one would not want to be in Nietzsche's position. Then I thought of E, the language man, the master of translation. I should have stopped myself at the start, the moment I suspected that my love for E might be unrequited. I don't like the idea of myself being dispensable in someone's life. But the truth is that I did not know what was happening here with me and E, in New York, and if it was something, what I was supposed to do in such circumstances. I was alone in America, but I would not and should not pretend I was really alone. My life in Britain had its presence in my everyday life here. I thought about how J would prepare food for our child, and how he would not notice her dirty school uniform or torn socks, and how late she might go to bed some nights.

Wedlock
婚约

A quote attributed to Alexandre Dumas père: 'The chain of wedlock is so heavy that it takes two to carry it – sometimes three.'

I thought of the child J and I have been bringing up. A child is more important than a marriage, perhaps. Marriage would mean little to me even if I were to carry that chain. But a child, yes, is a strong chain, almost unbreakable, though chain is not a 'positive' metaphor. For a woman, a child can be a home. This is especially so if you are an immigrant. For the immigrant, the child is a new root. The child grows in the soil where you find yourself, and ties you to that place, even if you are from somewhere else.

But what if a woman needs another kind of home, or wants to send out her own new roots? It is so much more difficult for her to acquire a certain freedom than a man. When money is not sufficient, and social support is scarce, how do we survive in this struggle between being a mother and being free to pursue creativity? A moral judgement condemns the woman who separates herself from her child, even if for a short while. A man can leave. He can sail around the world and he won't be judged. A man's identity is not defined in relation to a child or a woman, but to the world.

If childbearing and marriage define a certain woman's identity, then she is lucky. But this isn't how I identify myself. Especially, not here, not in America, where I had no history. Nor did anyone know my history.

America gave me this sense of potential. That potential we all have, but seldom activate.

And for some reason I thought of Lou Andreas-Salomé's life. Her relationship with Nietzsche was conditioned by her time, with its concepts of marriage as a religious sacrament and an economic arrangement. If not for all that, would Nietzsche and Salomé have ended up as lovers? Who knows? Maybe she did not love him that way. For him, her rejection was a deep wound, which sent him up into the mountain, and to his beloved *Übermensch*.

In contrast, Salomé moved on. Later she married a professor of linguistics, and lived in a secure but celibate marriage. She then met the young poet Rilke, and discovered sexual love at the age of thirty-seven. Freud was fascinated by her. She corresponded with Freud, and built her psychoanalyst career. She created her own freedom. She overcame what she had been.

But I was not Salomé. I was more like a patient in her clinic. I was a case study for her practice and her explorations of mental conflict. In this case, time had reversed. My analyst was in the past, and I was here, a woman living through a moment in the twenty-first century.

3
Radical: 言

(language, speech, words)

Cathay / China
契丹 / 中国

Old name for 'China' by Europeans. Originated from the
Chinese word 契丹 – Qìdān, or Khitan – the name of a nomadic
people who founded the Liao Dynasty around AD 916.

When I was still in England, J told me that when he was a child the
word 'Cathay' had sparked his imagination. It conjured up images of
an exotic kingdom, a land to which Marco Polo had travelled. For him
Cathay was not China.

The first time I came across this Western word Cathay was when
I noticed the airline Cathay Pacific, but I never wondered why it was
called this. 'Cathay' sounds to a Western ear like it might be a Chinese
word. But Chinese people can only tell if it is really a Chinese word once
they see it written down in *hanzi*. What is Cathay in Chinese script?
Westerners do not know. In any case Cathay sounds like an old colonial
official mispronouncing a Chinese word.

Indeed, Cathay originated from an old Chinese term – 契丹. In
Mandarin these characters are pronounced Qìdān, which in a roman-
ised form is Khitan. It was the name of a nomadic people in Central
East Asia. They moved towards the east 1,000 years ago, and founded
the Liao Dynasty in China. The dynasty then covered an area including
parts of Russia, North Korea, Mongolia and northern China. It was a
large territory but nothing compared to the later Yuan Dynasty, the
Mongol Empire, which was immense. This history reminds us of how
modern China came from a mix of cultures including a strong Muslim
tradition. But the process that led from the name Qìdān (Khitan) to

Cathay must have involved Europeans writing, translating and pro-
nouncing the words. By the time we get to Marco Polo in the 1300s, the
term Cathay is already being used. It appears in his book.

And how did Cathay become China? Was this another warped romanisation? There is a record of historical evolution in pronunciation
that takes us from Cathay to China. This record was created by European Jesuit missionaries and Western travellers. There is also the sug-
gestion that 'China' comes from the Sanskrit 'Cina', which was derived
from the name of the Chinese Qin Dynasty, pronounced 'Chin', which
was given as 'Cin' by the Persians. That transliteration seems to have
been popularised through trade along the Silk Road from China (Cina)
to the rest of the world.

But of course people who lived in China did not use the Western
alphabet then. For us, this is all a strange kind of morphing of sounds.
In the similar way that the English call plates and cups china. The story
is more about the speech impediments of foreigners than about how we
natives think of the name of our country. For us, China is designated
by the term 中国 (Zhong-guo). That means Middle Kingdom. The
concept is absolute and simple. It's an idea of world-centredness. It has
not been a shifting or elusive concept. It's like sticking your foot in the
ground or planting a tree. 'Cathay' and 'China' are strange ghost words
for us. Like smoke from a foreign cigar. Perfumed by meaninglessness.

Embalmed Animal
防腐动物

According to Borges, there exists 'a certain Chinese
encyclopedia' in which it is written that 'animals are divided
into: (a) belonging to the Emperor, (b) embalmed, (c) tame, (d)
sucking pigs . . .' (*Selected Non-Fictions*, Jorge Luis Borges)

The Argentinian writer Jorge Luis Borges became obsessed by China
and its language. He was captivated by ancient scripts. For him they
were mysterious signs from another world. Even if you look at his face
in photographs, Borges seems to have the physiognomy of a Manchu's
long, dour features, somewhat like a Hollywood actor made up to look
like a Mandarin in the court of Cixi, the last empress. Actually Borges
might have liked that idea. His obsession with ancient Chinese culture
overcame him when he was sixteen or seventeen years old. He decided
to dedicate himself to the study of oriental literature. This led him to
study the oldest songs of East Asia, *Shijing – Book of Odes*, verses from
3,000 years ago. The idea of the oldest songs, at least the ones written
down, is fascinating. But I don't believe in origins in this sense. There
are no 'first' or 'oldest' songs. Songs are as old as time. As long as there
have been people, there have been songs. But there is part of us that
always wants to find 'the first'. In his search for original meaning, Borges
looked at various translations and found them all puzzling. Each one
depicted something different. How was that possible? And which was
the true one? Where was the beautiful essence of past truth to be found?

  In Borges's search for the mysterious origins of meaning, he then
found the 'oldest encyclopedia', which I could not locate in Chinese.

And he wrote about it. But he did so in a fabulous way. Maybe his frustration with finding deep meaning led him to fabricate it. Another man, obsessed by meaning too, wrote about Borges's twist and turns. This was Foucault. He was fascinated by our struggle to understand the workings of a remote language. In his book *The Order of Things* he refers to Borges with a mixture of confusion and amusement:

> This [Borges] passage quotes a 'certain Chinese encyclopedia' in which it is written that 'animals are divided into: (a) belonging to the Emperor, (b) embalmed, (c) tame, (d) sucking pigs, (e) sirens, (f) fabulous, (g) stray dogs, (h) included in the present classification, (i) frenzied, (j) innumerable, (k) drawn with a very fine camelhair brush . . . In the wonderment of this taxonomy, the thing we apprehend in one great leap, the thing that, by means of the fable, is demonstrated as the exotic charm of another system of thought, is the limitation of our own.

I was intrigued. What was this crazy text? Belonging to the Emperor? Embalmed? And drawn with a very fine camelhair brush? I am Chinese and not uneducated, but I had never heard of any such strange writings. Sure, classical Chinese is an entirely different language. It has all the features Borges loved: obscure and complex, and at the same time vague and minimal. It's an enigmatic language pointing to meanings that we can now barely grasp. But I needed to take a break. Maybe look out the window at the Hudson. Or check out why there were police cars parked at the bottom of my building with their sirens blaring.

Erya

尔雅

The Erya is considered the earliest dictionary and encyclopedia in the world. Author unknown. It was created in the early Warring States, around 400 BC–200 BC.

So I went on my search. I spent quite some time online locating where Borges's quotation came from. Borges alleges it to be a fictitious taxonomy of animals based on 'a certain Chinese encyclopedia'. Those hints led me back to *Erya*. It has been claimed to be the earliest example of a dictionary and encyclopedia in the world. Normally, you would not find me doing anything like this. I usually dread reading anything more than three hundred years old. But here I was, brand new in America and gripped by a strange need to pull something ancient out of the past and into my present life.

The time-worn dictionary, I discovered, is divided into many sections; each section covers the lexicon of a specific domain, such as family, land, types of water, types of tree, birds, domestic animals and wild beasts, etc. And then I found it. There's a section entitled 'Interpreting

Beasts'. So, is this the entry of Borges's mythical encyclopedia? Here I'll try to put down my abridged, sketched (mis)translation. My purpose is simple. I want to contrast the translation in Borges's version – *'animals are divided into'* – with what I found in what I take to be the original. You may not understand these characters, but I want to include them, just to give a sense of the supposed original text, which might have entranced the fading eyes of Borges:

鹿牡麚牝麀其子麛其迹速绝有力鹿开
　狼牡貛牝狼其子獥绝有力迅
　兔子媆其迹远绝有力欣
　豕子猪豕豮豕羭幺幼羮者豕曶豕生三豵二师一特
　所寝橧四豴皆白豥

This will just look like Chinese script to you. But in fact a third of these characters are dead. The idiograms here lost their life centuries ago. They are fossils, but they might still tell us of their former life. There's also no punctuation, and the order of the characters is so strange. Were the text writers drunk, or were they guided by some ancient alien intelligence? After some struggle, I managed to dredge out the following:

Deer: a male deer is called Mu You; a female deer Pin You;

A young deer, its footprint is called Su; the strongest one is named Lu Kai.

Wolf: male wolf – Mu Huan; female wolf – Pin Lang; the cubs – Jiao – are aggressive.

Rabbit: Fan, its traces elusive; the fastest one among the young rabbits is called Xin.

Pig: boar, castrated boars, piglets.

Sows bearing three piglets are named Zong, two piglets are named Shi. Sows bearing one piglet named Te.

A grass-covered sty is called Zeng.

Pigs with four feet all white named Gai . . .

This section of the *Erya* uses the character for 'beasts':

The character is old. We don't use it in China any more. It's made up of many radicals. On the left you can see three mouths – 口, the radicals from the top to bottom resembling a gullet. On the right is the symbol of a dog: 犬. But this dog symbol is made up of a symbol of *big* 大 with a tear-like stroke on its shoulder. A big thing crying or barking must be a beast. The character, though obscure, takes us back to the lived experience of a wild, mountainside forest.

The text in this beast section refers to many animals: fox, hyena, bear, deer, leopard, white tiger, black tiger, and so on. But there were many signs for things I could not read. Perhaps that's where Borges's famous 'embalmed animals' were. Or 'the fabulous', or 'drawn with a very fine camelhair brush'. I made further attempts to decipher these signs. But I could make no headway. I believe that many scholars have attempted their own translations and some modern editions have been published. Still, we are all like an ancient human imagining life on the luminous moon.

I contemplated Borges's long Manchu face in the old photos. The eyes, I supposed, were brown. They were like dark pools, but framed by thick glasses. He was severely short-sighted, just like most Chinese people from the old days. He himself was a book of mysterious texts.

Some say the world out there is a text, and all we have to do is to translate this unknown language and to interpret it. But if this view were true, the world might be a text that defies translation. The world might be untranslatable. I wanted to talk to E about this, even though he does not understand Chinese.

Laconic

简洁

The word laconic – to speak in a concise way – is derived from
Laconia, a region in the Peloponnese in Greece. Throughout the
classical period the Laconia region was dominated by Spartans,
who were renowned for their verbal austerity and blunt remarks.

But weren't most ancient people laconic? To my knowledge the ancient
sages in the East were all concise. Great wisdom lies in great silence.
Go ask Buddha (but don't expect an answer). Lao Tzu and Zhuangzi
spoke so minimally that no one dared to claim they fully grasped their
mysterious sayings. The Japanese master Dogen Zenji meditated in
silence for most of his life. But modern-day leaders such as lawyers and
politicians have established the fact that to be laconic is to lose power.
Speak first and speak lengthily – these are the keys to success. Castro
could speak onstage for eighteen hours without a break, and Churchill
would only stop speaking when he had to puff on his cigar.

Even nowadays, when you go
to a Buddhist monk, and try to
ask about the meaning of life, or
death, you will get little in verbal
response. At most you might get
a glance from the man behind his
folding palms. That's what I got
decades ago, in a temple on the
side of a mountain, in Zhejiang
Province.

I also know that if I think and speak in Chinese, I become totally laconic. Especially if I picture the radicals with my mind's eye as I speak, I feel I do not need to say anything at all. Because it's all illustrated, vividly, in the flow of thought.

Empiricist

经验主义者

From Latin empeiria 'experience', based on peira 'trial, experiment'.

It is perhaps no longer possible to be an absolute empiricist. Our grandparents were probably more *empiricist* than people of our generation. We now live in an age in which we are all information rich and experience poor.

Empiricism is a philosophy that tells us that all knowledge comes from experience. A farmer or a fisherman is an empiricist in the sense that he or she uses agricultural knowledge gained through their own experience.

My favourite image of an empiricist is the Swedish botanist, zoologist and physician Carl Linnaeus. He was a near-perfect empiricist. He spent all his life collecting plants and classifying animals and minerals. He would not accept any categorisation if he had not personally experienced it, unless it was solidly grounded in his observations. In order to understand how tropical fruits might grow in cold northern landscapes, Linnaeus became the first man in Europe to induce a banana tree not only to sprout but also to bear fruit. I wonder how tall his banana tree was. What sort of joy did he experience in watching his plants finally blooming?

I have only seen flowering banana trees during my childhood in south China. I have never picked a banana with my hands. I am not quite an empiricist.

Plantain

芭蕉

From Spanish: plá(n)tano.

I am not sure whether Linnaeus's banana plant was a plantain or a banana. If it was a plantain, then its fruit should have been harvested green and used in cooking. For Europeans, banana plants have always been exotic, just like the flora and fauna in Henry Rousseau's paintings.

Back in our London apartment, just before my departure, I was packing my clothes and sorting out my luggage. When I came into the kitchen, J was chopping a plantain by a heated pan. His thesis on Nietzsche was lying beside the chopping board, smeared with butter. Then he turned to me, and said:

'Does this remind you of something?'

I looked at him, and smiled. 'A banana?'

'Something else?'

I nodded. 'Your penis?'

'I knew you had something on your mind. Do you want to eat some when it's fried?'

'Yes, with your balls too.'

We both laughed. And it was me who ate most of the fried plantain in the end, even though he was the one who had wanted it. Shortly after that day, I left for America. And some months after that, I met E the linguist who was also a fervent follower of Linnaeus.

Ellipsis
省略号

From Greek elleipein, 'leave out'.

No country for old men. No winter for southerners.

Winter in New York was tough. Though it was not as grey as it is in London. But it was cold. When it was chilly and sunless, solitude was no longer a virtue to bear. Sometimes, in the afternoon, the sun appeared after a grey morning. And I would sit in my room by the window, bathed in the warmth of the afternoon light, reading, or floating around in my thoughts, transfixed by the static flow of the Hudson River under my window. How long would this light last?

An hour later, I was still in the same black leather chair. My body had been warmed up. Loneliness had been replaced by longing. All I was thinking about now was E.

I wrote to him. There were only a few lines, each had very few words. Every line started 'I' and rushed to an ellipsis.

I . . .

I need . . .

I want . . .

He didn't come to see me, even though he lived nearby. Instead, he answered, after two hours:

'Don't use so many ellipsis. I can't understand anything you've written with all these dots!'

He said he would see me that night, but the last line from him insisted: 'How am I supposed to understand a sentence that has only "I" then just an ellipsis?'

I should not have written to him, or have written anything. But saying nothing was different from using many ellipsis. No, the plural is ellipses. (How can ellipsis have a singular form and a plural one? Is this some pedantic Western grammar again? They are just dots. Only dots!) Yes, saying nothing to him was just *nothing*; using ellipses helped me to say a lot, by not saying. I could not express my enormous need for him.

I recalled reading the 'real' Whitman in his 'real' language, and discovering that he used so many ellipses – at least those dots were everywhere in his first edition. *Perfume . . . my mouth . . . I am in love with it . . .*

In Chinese, punctuation wasn't used until relatively recently, and we didn't adopt Western punctuation until the 1920s. I don't think I have encountered an ellipsis in any Chinese text produced before the Cultural Revolution. How often did I use an ellipsis in my Chinese writing? Not often, perhaps. Not at all. My Chinese compositions, stories and poems – those seem a long time ago. In Chinese script, an ellipsis had six dots. So that our poor short-sighted Chinese people (including myself) can see them more clearly. The six-dotted ellipses in Chinese texts are perhaps even more ambiguous. So much unsaid. So much suggested!

Juzi
桔子

Chinese citrus such as oranges, mandarins or clementines.

I ate two juzi. What do the people here call this fruit? Oranges? Or clementines? No, the Americans call them mandarins. Just like the name they give to an imperial Chinese civil servant. All these strange labels. One can't be totally Linnaeus about everything, otherwise we would all live like accountants gathering spreadsheets throughout our lives. For me these are just citrus trees that bear white flowers. Most of them originate in ancient China, where they existed long before other cultures came along to name them.

I picked up Walt Whitman again. I read each line slowly, as though for the first time: the perfume, the mouth, the lilac trees, being naked by the riverbank. I pictured Whitman with or without a beard, but with a spontaneous erection in the bushes. Erections – plural, multiple. And what bushes? Bushes on the east coast of nineteenth-century America. Yes, I felt these elements from each line. But I could not understand them. Almost none of them. Once again, I felt I was back in that comedy club in England, everyone there laughing and clapping but me.

Punctuation

标点

From medieval Latin punctus (n-).

Once upon a time, *jadis* . . . there was neither writing nor punctuation. Claws made scratches here and there in caves. Images were the reality; the lions on the wall were the lions seen the day before. Then the claws grasped some tools: a stone, a stick, a knife, then a pen. As the knife became sharper, the stone more angular and the pen found paper, the world changed.

The Chinese writing system has come a long way in its evolution. Perhaps around the time of World War I there was a crucial turning point. East and West were in a state of intense friction and discord. After WWI the revolutionaries in Beijing looked upon the Western world and realised that the Chinese language needed to be modernised, and that would include the writing system. We stopped writing *hanzi* from top to bottom, or from right to left. We threw away our brushes and calligraphic art, we adopted the romanisation for our characters. We followed the rules from the 'civilised world'.

But this is not a unique story. Many ancient writing cultures had neither punctuation nor spacing. If he had to engrave words on a hard piece of bamboo, or on a turtle shell, a scribe might as well use the limited space to say as much as possible. Apparently, the oldest known document using punctuation is the Mesha Stele from the ninth century BC in the Middle East. Around the fifth century BC the Greeks were sporadically using vertically arranged dots – usually two (dicolon) or three (tricolon) – as an aid in the oral delivery of texts. But after all these centuries, dots have become a science and an art, as typography has become a science and a pop art.

Nowadays, there are even two new punctuation marks: 'question comma': ؟ and 'exclamation comma': ¡ These are intended for use within a sentence, a function for which the normal question and exclamation marks are ill-suited. I wonder why not just use emojis? Aren't they more expressive? If computers had come before punctuation, we would have used emojis instead of all these dots and marks!

Carnegie Hall
卡内基音乐厅

A concert hall in Midtown Manhattan in New York City.

I saw a poet sitting in front of the New York Public Library, selling his books.

I went to Bryant Park twice that week. One time it was to eat my lunch among the flower beds; the second time I went to the library to look at the catalogues. And there he was, the poet in the park, under the noon sun as well as in the glow of dusk. He was in his forties, wore a faded shirt, and had a humble manner. There was a homeless feel about him, despite a certain nobleness he exuded. A handwritten sign in front of his little table read: *Meet the author.* Some passers-by stopped for a few seconds, leafing through his books. Others went by, as if he were a tree, or a bush at the bottom of the library steps. He was part of the library and Bryant Park.

I was a little surprised by his presence. It seemed to me that not everyone could place a table and a chair in front of such an institution in Manhattan without being hassled by the police. Did he have such charm that the guards took pity on him and left him in peace?

A week later, I saw him again. I went over and looked at his work, carefully laid out on the table. He welcomed my curiosity with a warm and innocent smile. His smile was childlike, uncorrupted. The rare innocence of his face made me almost sad. I began to talk to him.

'All my books are self-published, like Walt Whitman!' That's the first thing he said to me. I was impressed by his instant association with the saint, my Whitman. I asked where he was originally from. He said he grew up in Alabama, which explained his accent. Alabama! I exclaimed, trying to visualise the American map in my head.

'Whitman is my hero,' the poet said, again with a warm and innocent smile. 'I feel very connected to him. I left school when I was a teenager, and Waltman, he left formal schooling when he was twelve. We are both self-taught and self-published!'

I congratulated him, and asked if I could film him. He agreed. I took out my phone and recorded him reciting a poem about his mother. His verses were simple and natural. At the end of the poem, I thought I saw tears in his eyes. Well, perhaps I did not see the tears, but there was a change in his voice. It suddenly became small, and suppressed. A stone in his throat. He had to stop, and he fell briefly into silence.

I spent a bit more time with the poet, Mr Robinson. His name was printed on the covers of his various books. He told me he had been homeless for a while, and now he commuted, every day, from a lodge outside of New York City. I could not make out the town he mentioned. But he said he liked to be stationed in Bryant Park. 'It's good for me, this commuting life.'

The last thing he talked about was how much he loved ballet, and the famed dancer Martha Graham, though he mentioned Graham in an elusive way. As I was leaving, he mentioned Carnegie Hall, and how much he hoped to see a show there one day, for real. I walked away, past the carrousel on the lawn, and thought of Carnegie Hall where I had never been. My encounter with Mr Robinson felt like a scene from the last century, or even the century before. An encounter with a kind of life we have decisively abandoned, along with poetry. I heard Whitman chanting in my ears. *O Captain my Captain, our fearful trip is done, and the ship has weathered every rack . . .*

Paraphrased
释义

Latin, from Greek paraphrasis, paraphrazein, para- 'expressing modification' + phrazein 'tell'.

Alone in America, I had plenty of time. No child to interrupt my concentration every five minutes, no family duties to which I must submit myself at any moment. I could even watch old films, by the Maysles Brothers or Godard, in Harlem Library. One afternoon, after having some more garbanzo beans, I tried to borrow Godard's *Made in U.S.A.*, but the DVD did not work. Instead, I found a recent Godard film: *Goodbye to Language.* I thought I would like to understand more about language, though maybe Godard meant the visual language. It was a 3D movie and I did not have the special glasses with which to watch it. The images were blurred. But I sat through it nevertheless.

I felt that through those raw and chaotic images, Godard was trying to discuss the treachery of language. Or, the fragility and unreliability of verbal language, and the death of classical images. Perhaps that was one of the reasons he made a 3D movie at the age of eighty-four, to illustrate that defeat, verbally and visually. For sure, Godard has been disappearing from the public view in the last two decades, or more.

As always, the master had to quote great literature. Sometimes he even quoted himself, something he had said half a century ago. In *Adieu au langage*, he paraphrased many authors and books: Guillaume Apollinaire's *Alcools*, Louis Aragon's *Elsa, je t'aime*, Samuel Beckett's *The Image*, Borges's *The Book of Sand*, and Flaubert, Dostoevsky, as well as Freud. There is even a slogan from Mao Zedong – a curious comment about the French Revolution: 'Too early to tell!', or was that actually from the premier, Zhou Enlai?

For this very book I am writing now, and that you are reading now, one of the only ways to quote classics is to paraphrase. How can I quote other dictionaries, when I'm trying to create my own? With languages and cultures, I am under a vast weight that precedes me. It's a burden on my own words. How can I progress? Why don't I just walk away, and not speak? Maybe one day I will. Give up words. Though not quite like the aged Godard. For now, I must continue, with an inexplicable compulsion.

Mandarin
普通话

Standard Chinese speech in mainland China. It also means the imperial exam system for officials in ancient China.

'Mandarin' is not a Chinese word. I have always found it strange – you would think it's a truly Chinese word, but we don't use it.

Mandarin has two meanings. It can mean the main language spoken in China. It also means a certain kind of bureaucrat in the Chinese civil service.

Obviously, Mandarin is a Western word. It was invented by Portuguese missionaries around the sixteenth century. First, the official language in China is Putong Hua – standard speech. Secondly, our name for a civil servant of the imperial times is *guan ren* – official man, or educated man.

The word mandarin morphed from the Portuguese *mandarim*. It was used in the sixteenth century during the time when the Portuguese physician Tomé Pires was in Ming China. Pires was the first Western man to launch a foreign embassy in imperial China, though the Ming emperor never received him in person. After all, only a few years before Pires arrived in China on a fleet in 1514, the Portuguese carried out the conquest of Malacca. And the Chinese were suspicious of the white man's intentions. The embassy was dissolved a few years later, with some of its members killed by the locals. Tomé Pires himself became ill and died in China.

The Portuguese word was thought by many to be related to *mandador*: one who commands, and *mandar*: to command. But some scholars believe that the word came from the Sanskirt *mantri*, meaning minister or counsellor. In any case, for the European missionaries and travellers from the sixteenth century onwards, it was logical to call the language of the officials the 'Mandarin language', translating the Chinese name *Guanhua*.

I spoke Mandarin when I went to Beijing for university. But I am not sure if I really understand the Mandarin examination system of imperial China. In our schooldays, we read many poems and prose pieces about the sad fate of those who failed their imperial exams. Many educated men aspired to the highest service and submitted themselves to rigorous study for years, and then sat the tests, only to fail and indeed fail repeatedly. In the end all these poor souls could do was drink by the edge of a lake, calling out with nostalgia to their absent women. Though of course some did succeed, such as the celebrated Tang Dynasty poet Du Fu. Certainly, Du was a genius. If you have read his work, you will know that most of his poems are about savage wars and the sorrows of a drifting life. The imperial court seemed to be always far away from the poet's life. Even the emperor of Du Fu's time was in exile. Life was a mournful succession of passing events, whether one was a noble imperial servant or a humble farmer in the fields, let alone a lonely alcoholic poet. Perhaps that's where Taoism and Buddhism gain their space for the mind. All desires are falling petals, all things are passing wind.

Roget's Thesaurus
罗杰词典

Written by the English physician and lexicographer Peter Mark
Roget (1779–1869), it was published in 1852. The original edition
had 15,000 words. Roget's schema of classification is based on
the philosophical work of the seventeenth-century German
polymath Gottfried Wilhelm Leibniz.

Peter Mark Roget struggled with depression for most of his life. The
thesaurus arose partly from an effort to battle it. When Roget was eight
years old, he was already obsessed with list-making. Some biographers
believe it was his way of coping with his troubled childhood. This characteristic behaviour is very close to that of Dr Samuel Johnson. Johnson's obsession with lexicons was some sort of physical attempt to deal
with depression and a life deprived of sensuality.

Roget was a chess player. He devised chess problems, and designed
an inexpensive pocket chessboard. I wonder if there is a link between
the lexicographer and the chess player, in terms of organising, control-
ling and making order.

When I was young, I was fascinated by 圍棋 – the game of Go.
For me, it was not so much about order and control, but more about
its aesthetic simplicity. I loved those round, black and white stones,
and the philosophy of death by encirclement. Life seems to be simple
in a Go game: to survive is to leave your path unobstructed, and your
surroundings open.

I like sometimes to picture myself as a lexicographer or an etymolo-
gist, but not with the ambition and style of Roget. Neatness does not

belong to my book, nor list-making and rigid definitions. Like a Go
player with words, I like to free words up from their surroundings,
and to leave the doors of meaning unlocked, the furnishing of the
house incomplete, and allow my verbal garden to overgrow. I welcome
plenty of synonyms and antonyms, foreign words and words that matter to women. Like a verbal bricoleur I like the words of many tongues,
because no single voice can command all meanings.

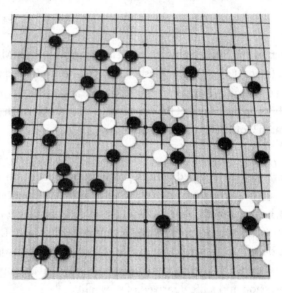

4
Radical: 气
(qi, energy, spirit)

Eros

性爱

Latin, from Greek, literally 'sexual love'.

One would think that 'romantic love' is *natural*, as natural as the need to eat and to drink. It must have existed from the beginning of human history. But the more I read about it, the less I believe this theory. I am not sure what the difference is between *eros* and *romantic love*. Or are they just different terms for one reality? The invention of 'romantic love' is almost like the invention of an ideology. The idea seems to be as much of a construct as the concept of marriage, loyalty or devotion. According to Joseph Campbell's *The Power of Myth*, our concept of romantic love began in twelfth-century Europe. Before then, according to Campbell, love was simply *Eros*, the god who excites your sexual desire.

Why did the idea of romantic love arise then? What happened in twelfth-century Europe? Looking at the historical timeline, we learn that the Duke of Normandy returned from the First Crusade, and invaded England in an attempt to take the throne from his brother, Henry I. What else happened then? The University of Bologna was founded in 1140, one of the oldest universities in the world. But what about events in Asia, Africa and America? Are we to believe that Mayans or Incans or ancient Chinese were unable to fall in love romantically, and were purely driven by the reproductive imperative? And what about the ancient Greeks – the myths of Aphrodite, Venus and Cupid?

In Ovid's *Metamorphoses*, there is this paragraph: 'Once, when Venus' son [Eros] was kissing her, his quiver dangling down, a jutting arrow, unbeknown, grazed her breast. She pushed the boy away. In fact the wound was deeper than it seemed, though unperceived at first. And she became enraptured by the beauty of a man [Adonis].'

How should we define the meaning of eros? Ancient people conceptualised eros in all sorts of ways, as humans always do, imagining strange creatures, plants, objects and natural elements. The paradox of any definition is that once we define a concept, we lose other possibilities. That's why we have to return to myths. Myths are where we look to find meanings or definitions. Yes, once upon a time, *jadis*.

Frictions
摩擦力

There are four types of friction: static, sliding, rolling and fluid friction. Static friction is strongest – for example, a heated iron on materials such as fabric or wood.

Of course, I know, and E knows, our love began from eros, though it was suppressed at the beginning. I was not *really* free. My mind was never free. I projected my yearning onto the space around us, onto New York City. Some intensified energy had been floating in parks, in cinemas, as well as on those paths by the Hudson and East River. This energy eventually gathered and consumed in the bedroom.

What is friction, though? It produces heat, that's one of its characteristics. In order for us not to be burned, the friction between us had to find a release.

I felt that when we first began to discover each other, the friction between us resulted from our different ways of life. We behaved differently in almost everything. E treated the relationship cautiously as part of the management of daily life, whereas I behaved in the opposite way. There was no tomorrow, I said to myself, today was the day and we must not wait. Make love either now or never. Friction is a Western word. I thought of a Chinese expression – 情结, love knot. But love knot did not seem to describe our moments together. And, in reality, it felt the love knot between us generated battles, mistrust and anxiety. But it was impossible to untie this love knot when we were still physically together.

Semen

精液

From Latin, literally 'seed', from serere 'to sow'.

I read recently about research conducted by two English scientists, Dr Baker and Dr Bellis. They tried to find out why the human penis must ejaculate 350 million sperm when a man has no intention of fertilising 350 million women. They attribute it to a theory of sperm competition. The theory holds that sperm must be prepared to do battle with the sperm of another man inside a woman, given the possibility that she has 'double mated'.

Evolution seems to tell a truth denied by civilisation. How many millions of spermatozoa are good and how many are bad? Maybe only one is good. Maybe none.

In Chinese, semen is *jingye* – the spirited liquid. It sounds a little mysterious, and perhaps more positive? In Tibetan tantric Buddhism, sexual practice is welcomed as part of the path to enlightenment. But tantric Buddhists believe that men should not ejaculate. They believe that 'the spirited liquid' enhances man's energy – qi – and allows him to channel it towards spiritual realisation. This reminds me of what Balzac said about his writing life. He once said that he lost a novel in a particular morning, because he had allowed himself to come before he got up. One wonders how many more novels he could have written if he had not allowed any of his seed to be scattered.

Hymen
元红

Hymen is a membrane which partially closes the opening of the vagina. From Greek humēn, 'membrane'.

In Samuel Johnson's dictionary, under the word *hymen*, we read: 1. *The god of marriage.* 2. *The virginal membrane.* Whether a woman likes it or not, it seems that the concepts of marriage and virginity have always been linked. How lowly and primitive it is that we presume the value of marriage to be manifested in that thin piece of tissue.

In Milton's *Paradise Lost*, the two concepts are again wedded in Adam and Eve's bodily pleasures:

> *With flowers, garlands, and sweet-smelling herbs*
> > *Espoused Eve deckt first her nuptial bed,*
> > *And heavenly quires the hymenæan sung . . .*

Why am I thinking about this word, an almost dead word? Of course, the intactness of the hymen is traditionally taken to be a mark of virginity. Seldom do I encounter the word in my current life. It sounds imposed, and strangely archaic. But I can imagine that if I travelled in a remote area in China, I might overhear gossip from the locals, talk between farmers, and among women in the fields, about proof of virginity and broken tissues, and blood on sheets.

In traditional Chinese literature, the hymen is present only in a metaphorical word: *yuanhong* – 元红: prime red. Or sometimes, it is *luohong* – 落红: falling red. It's only in the last half-century that the

Chinese language has added a scientific term: *chu nu mo* – 处女膜: virginal membrane.

As for my own hymen, I don't have any sense of its loss. The dull wound or the joyful opening? Which perspective should I take, now that I am distant from my chaotic past and youth? When (in which event) did it become a *falling red*? Did I ever notice the particular moment of that *prime red* on a bedsheet, or was it rather on a street corner? Or on a bench at the back of a classroom? I cannot recall having seen any rusty stain, though I can recall multiple physical pains during those years.

Spittoon (Sputum) Theory of Womanhood
痰盂女性化理论

A 1971 documentary by D. A. Pennebaker captured the infamous
debate between Germaine Greer and Norman Mailer in New
York. Greer bashed Mailer's theory of lovemaking, calling it the
Spittoon Theory of Womanhood.

What got me thinking about hymens was thinking about Germaine
Greer.

Pennebaker's footage of Mailer and Greer's debate in 1971 is on You-
Tube and has been widely watched. It shows a typically patriarchal take
on men's sexual orientation towards women: 'When a man makes love
with a woman, he empties out all his good and his bad into her.' Greer
fights back: 'This is the spittoon theory of womanhood. Sexual politics
has something to do with the act of fucking, being to the advantage of
the one who fucks, and to the disadvantage of the one who is fucked.
And the one who is fucked, be it male or female, goat or pig, or stone,
is always characterised as female and inferior.'

I thought of a spittoon. In sepia-stained pictures of the old days,
usually a spittoon is an elongated saucer in a bar, for spitting into.
It's a grotesque picture when one colours it with brown foamy liquid
extruded from a tobacco-stuffed mouth. In Greer's spittoon theory the
vagina is the receptacle for the ejaculate of the rutting male. 'When a
man makes love to a woman, he empties all his good and his bad into
her.' Greer could no longer take such sexualised language from men,
especially when that language was dressed up in the debased speech
of sentimentality. That kind of language has been abundantly spewed

by male authors throughout our literary history – indeed, not only in literary history, but everywhere in our daily discourse.

I also thought of Greer's controversial speech about rape. In the seventies and eighties she told *Playboy* magazine and other media about how she was raped at the age of nineteen. She claimed she was not actually hurt by the intrusion of the man's penis but more by the man's fists and violent mind. Her remarks caused outrage among feminists. For me, she was misunderstood. Her point was not to glorify the power of penis, but to lay down the mere fact that violence comes from male minds and the male society.

Jackson Heights
杰克逊高地

A neighbourhood in Queens in *NYC*, with half of its population being foreign-born.

It is a long train ride from Harlem to Queens. But still, I often went. I felt a certain homecoming in Jackson Heights. It is a neighbourhood of aggression and reception. In Jackson Heights, near the main bus station, there is a pedestrianised square I would stroll through. It is named Diversity Plaza. A strangely official name for such a seedy place, as if it was an official square for the Communist Party. This area is known for its Himalayan community, mixed with Latinos and Caribbeans as well as almost every ethnic group one can find in New York. One afternoon, I was walking down the street when I noticed a woman following close behind. She approached me and said: 'You look special, your energy is vibrating.' She added: 'I can feel it from you!'

I stared at her in puzzlement. She was in her fifties, with dark curly hair. Her plump body was wrapped in a red-and-yellow robe. Her fingers were covered with rings, and her wrist with silver bangles. I didn't know how to respond to her. Then she repeated the same thing again.

I wondered what she wanted from me. My hand pressed into my bag.

'Don't you want me to tell you what your future holds?' She smiled, in her forceful and blunt manner.

'And how much do I have to pay you for that?' was my answer.

She raised two fingers. 'Twenty dollars.'

I shook my head and walked away. Again she followed me, tight like my shadow. I passed a fruit store, then a few clothes shops. 'Listen, you've got a very special spirit. Your energy is strong. Don't you want to know what's going to happen?'

I pushed ahead, moving as fast as I could. Passing a traffic light, I headed straight to the subway station. Once I crossed the street, the woman behind me slowed down. It looked like she wanted to remain in her territory.

'How much can you pay? Fifteen dollars?' was her last attempt, shouting out from the other side of the street.

I shrugged, smiled back.

I didn't really want to leave Jackson Heights. So I descended the stairs of the subway and came up again on the other side. By then, the woman with many rings and bangles had disappeared. Your energy is vibrating, I told myself. I could feel it.

Periwinkle

长春花

1. An old-world plant with five-petalled flowers and glossy leaves.

   Genera Vinca and *Catharanthus*, family Apocynaceae.

2. A small herbivorous shore-dwelling mollusc with a spiral shell.

That day, on the way back from Jackson Heights, I took a walk around Flushing Meadow. I saw pink and blue periwinkles in the park. Hot pink. Purple blue. All blooming. I knew these flowers, from my old worlds, from China, and from England. They are the kind of flowers associated with old people and sadness. I stared at them for a while, and realised that I was in a neighbourhood I knew nothing of. Neither its history nor its present. Only the occasional passing Chinese family reminded me that I was in America.

Periwinkles. I thought of old wet England, my adopted country. I thought of a poem by the war poet Edward Thomas:

There once the walls
Of the ruined cottage stood.
The periwinkle crawls
With flowers in its hair into the wood.

For Edward Thomas, they were the everlasting flowers that would blossom in abandoned landscapes. They live to tell the tale of death and sorrow. I also remember, from a piece of folklore I read somewhere, that if one stares at a periwinkle flower long enough one can restore lost memories. Perhaps I would have to do this at some point in my life, stare at one of these blue flowers, in order to regain my past or even to regain my original language.

In Chinese, periwinkle is *chang chong hua* – everlasting spring flower.

Nicotine

尼古丁

An addictive pale-brown-coloured or colourless oily chemical
which constitutes the essence of tobacco.

A honeybee can smell a particular flower or toxin two kilometres away.
So can a butterfly. A dog can smell an object or person as far as fifteen
kilometres away, and can distinguish a vast variety of different odours.
We humans are not that sensitive to smells compared with animals.

I felt that I had known E's scent before, when I kissed him. His lips,
his mouth. They had the taste of wine, and were somehow a little salty.
His mouth – slightly sweet and salty. But when I kissed the slightly
wrinkled skin on his arms, I thought about someone else. Someone
far away from us, in another country, in another language, had almost
the exact same taste.

It's the taste of nicotine. A particular brand.

I don't smoke. I would not know which brand it was. I would never
have asked E. A strange thing to ask. We never asked about each other's
family and background. We knew that neither of us was 'free'. He had
his family dependants, though they lived in another city. So did I. Neither of us was a free-floating individual. Then perhaps none of the
passers-by in the streets of Harlem were free-floating individuals. None
of the residents of Jackson Heights either. None of us lived the way I
like to imagine Whitman did. *O brother, where are you?*

Verrazzano–Narrows Bridge
韦拉扎诺 - 窄桥

A suspension bridge in New York City connecting Staten Island
and Brooklyn. The span is named for Giovanni da Verrazzano,
the first documented European explorer to enter New York
Harbor and the Hudson River, in 1524.

I was right next to the Verrazzano Bridge, with my video camera. I was
planning to get to Staten Island to do some filming. 'Don't go there, it's
just some cops living there and it's rough,' a New Yorker warned me.
But that was exactly what I needed. Filming cops would be thrilling for
a Chinese person, something we could not do in PRC. While waiting
for a taxi, the Bee Gees song 'Night Fever' rang in my ears and images
from *Saturday Night Fever* started to play in my mind.

I saw John Travolta as Tony, a young Italian American hanging out with his gang on the bridge. Cars and water rush past under their feet, they dance and shout, trying to escape a dull working-class life. The fancy nightlife in the discotheque where Tony dances does not seem to change his daytime life. He always has to go back to work in the paint shop. But this bridge is a playground, a refuge, for young Tony to escape his family and his wretched reality, until one day, his friend falls from this very bridge and dies.

The water was blue, and indeed narrow. I looked down and beyond. The Statue of Liberty was far away in the distance. It began to rain, and I had discovered some problems with my camera. Taxis passed me without stopping. I was stuck next to this enormous steel bridge. All I wanted in the dirty rain was to get back to Manhattan. I could jump on the subway, into a graffiti-smeared carriage, just like Tony had done more than forty years ago, hoping to be received by his lover in the morning, in a bright Manhattan apartment.

Sedentary

久坐

From Latin sedatus, past participle of sedare 'settle', from sedere 'sit'.

New York in early spring was still frozen, and the central heating in E's apartment was lukewarm. He could not control the temperature, he explained.

A few afternoons, waiting for the snow to stop, I felt trapped in his place. Then, two weeks before my departure, I said to him jokingly: 'In case I ever return to this apartment, will you buy a heater? Just for me.'

To my surprise, the following day, a small new radiator appeared in the living room. It sent out a warm and gentle air, from the floor up to my legs.

'It was star reviewed by the *New York Times*, so I trusted it,' E said proudly.

I didn't know he could be so domestic, or adaptable. I had thought that E knew more about the language of animals than the language of daily life. Birds, insects, plants – these are the things he read about every day. But now it was different, he had bought a heater, and was buying a new desk for me.

I could see that in spite of our nostalgia for nature and wildness we prefer to live a comfortable urban life. We have clung to domestic and sedentary comfort, which will eventually kill us.

Flux

波动／流动

From Latin fluxus, from fluere 'to flow'.

The Greek philosopher Heraclitus was an almost perfect Taoist, if I look at it from an Eastern point of view. Flux is his word. Everything flows and nothing abides.

All is flux, nothing stays still. Just as he claimed that one cannot stand in the same water twice. Though the concept of 'sameness' is questionable. Where did he get the idea that anything in the world should be the 'same' as anything else?

Heraclitus said the sun is new every day. In the morning when I wake up in my bed – but which bed? which space? The sun that rises above the Hudson River in Upper Manhattan is not the same sun that is above Hackney Wick in London. So, I should think differently, every day, about love, about E and J, in relation to our families (their existence precedes us).

Let's say the old sage is right, every day there is newness. But something new can also mean an eruption, a breaking apart, total chaos. I am not sure where this chaos will lead me. I did not know about it then, and I still do not know now.

5

Radical: 色

(sex, colour, beauty)

Eros vs Aphrodite

爱神 vs 阿芙罗狄蒂

Eros is the Greek god of love and sex. Aphrodite is the Greek
goddess of love, pleasure and beauty.

For some reason, I find it difficult to say 'That is erotic' about a situation
or a feeling. That's not because I never have feelings or find myself in
situations that one might call 'erotic'. Rather, it's because for me, the
expression 'erotic' sounds male. The god of love and sex for the Greeks
was Eros. He was a man. But the Greeks had Aphrodite too, the female
goddess of love, pleasure and passion. Why do we say 'erotic' to express
our sexual feelings and responses, rather than 'aphrodisiacal'? Are we
just using the male position to describe sexual passion?

We understand that an aphrodisiac can generate and induce sexual desire – eros. But still, this is male. The aphrodisiac is the means
or cause of sexual passion, or the object of passion. That's Aphrodite.
Women are the aphrodisiac, men are the experiencers of passion.

The Chinese word for aphrodisiac medicine or food is 春药 – *chun
yao*. It literally means spring medicine. The topic of spring medicine has
been taboo in Chinese society. In an old fable – Legend of the White
Snake – a young man falls in love with a beautiful lady in white without
knowing her true identity as a snake spirit. A jealous and vicious monk
sends a bottle of sorghum wine mixed with arsenic to the young man,
so that when the lady drinks the wine she shows her true nature. She
becomes sexual and loses her control, turning back into a snake. The
man sees the snake and is so horrified that he dies from shock. Lessons

to learn: a woman should never drink aphrodisiac medicines! It will turn her into a dangerous animal.

Most of our moral stories are entrenched in the patriarchal tradition, just as the word 'erotic' is charged with the male position. One has to live with the tradition whether one wants to launch a language revolution or not. The word 'woman' is a variation on 'man'. It reflects a male orientation. And don't forget the Chinese character for 'woman' 女, a kneeling female. Eradicating the prejudicial aspects of language could be viewed as a form of censorship. As far as I can see, nearly every language has sexist terms. So where do we go from here? My thinking is that we should use the existing vocabularies but deploy artistic licence to play with them, rather like a creative calligrapher plays with traditional characters – swirling the inked brush to reflect their inner being.

Autoerotism

自我性恋

Auto + erotism. The *Merriam-Webster Dictionary* defines autoerotism as 'sexual feelings arising without external stimulation'. There is no equivalent word in Chinese.

When we think of sex, we think of stimulation by another. But there is also autoerotism, stimulation by oneself.

Here is my thinking about falling in love. When we fall in love with someone, it can be seen as an autoerotic act. It is falling in love with the idea of a good self – I see the idealistic self in the desired person – that's how the person in love functions. Hence the desire to embrace the body and the mind of the loved one.

Sugar Plum Fairy

糖梅仙子

The Sugar Plum Fairy is a character from Tchaikovsky's ballet *The Nutcracker*. She is the ruler of the Land of Sweets, and the character is danced by a prima ballerina.

From the north-west side of Central Park, E and I walked through the dusk all the way to a hotel on the east side. We needed a drink.

The hotel had been renovated, E remarked, walking across the plush carpet of the lobby. He said that he often met people in hotel bars. I didn't ask with whom he had come here in the past. The lounge was in the back, with a few impressionistic paintings on the wall. We sat by the bar, as he always preferred, and looked at the drinks menu.

I remember most of the drinks on the menu were from Russian ballets and operas. I ordered a Sugar Plum Fairy. I cannot remember what E ordered. Will he tell me, one day, when he has read this book?

By the time our drinks arrived, we were longing to be alone to touch each other. But we were muted and almost trapped, in that public space. His lips were close to my hair. I didn't sit on my stool. I stood by his, with my back to him. I felt him behind my hips. My neck was against his chest. He smelled faintly of nicotine. Somehow he refrained from kissing me. There were other guests in the lobby. Not many, but two other tables were occupied. That was too exposed for him, I guessed.

I sipped the Sugar Plum Fairy. It was a strange cocktail, sweet and spicy, not too strong, with two marshmallows on top. I bit into a marshmallow; it was too perfumy for my taste. Under the bartender's curious but persistent gaze, we didn't speak much. While feeling the warmth from his body, I wondered about the fairies in *The Nutcracker*, and the amorous tension between us.

I never went back to that hotel.

Crymax
高潮中的流泪

Cry as in 'cli' + max.

When reaching an orgasm, very often, tears well up in my eyes. Come and tears seem to be a whole bodily reaction to the extremity of love. I crymax, to relieve a massive, sweet pain. Though 'sweet' is a strange word, not one that comes naturally to me. It's more a thing that a man would say to a woman. Still, pain is the essence of that act. Joyful pain, or painful joy?

But with E, I realised I had never done that. Why? Perhaps we had not known each other long enough. The absence of deep trust. There was a certain resistance in me, even when I was in his arms and he was inside me. This self-control wouldn't let me come or cry. Was it partly because we were still learning to understand each other, to understand our physical languages? Of course, the heart of the matter is that we were together for only several weeks, not even months. (Is that true? How is that possible?) During my first few months in New York, I had spent my time wandering along the Hudson River, reading and scribbling away, occasionally observing small crabs swimming by the bank. I hadn't met him then. With a little longing and melancholy, I embraced my aloneness. Meeting E didn't remove my loneliness. It actually sharpened it, and made me realise how much I wanted to be embraced, by the other, by the loved one.

Clouds and Rains
云雨

A Chinese idiom, 云雨之欢 , to express the sexual joy between
a man and a woman. It was prevalent in the Ming Dynasty
classics, for example *The Golden Lotus*.

It was never easy, or it never came naturally with E. Our lovemaking
was like trying to find a language in order to communicate better.

We didn't really speak the same kind of language. He was patient,
and I was hasty. His body was a ruin, he said, just as D. H. Lawrence
wrote in his essays about England, though E was not an Englishman.
Men's and women's bodies are the ruins of our civilisation, Lawrence
wrote, as he left Britain with Frieda, his German lover, whom he married in 1914. Our sexuality has been twisted, our bodies are dead. To *feel*
oneself is to be reborn from the ruins of prudishness and suppression.
Yes, my body is like that, E confessed, D. H. Lawrence was talking about
my kind of body, my kind of culture.

But still, we wanted each other. Who could refuse life when it
offered itself to us, like a gift? My ankles crossed. He entered me. I
touched his pubic bone, which was warm against my clitoris. I could
have touched his penis, very gently. But I didn't. He would have come,
quickly.

Another time, on the same day, but in the evening. I felt warm and
wet again. He brought me to the edge of the bed. I needed a position. I
rested my hip and an arm on one side, and pressed my thighs together.
He stood, and took me from behind.

But time was running out. Simply, we had to leave each other. His family was calling him. And mine too, calling me from London. The pandemic, which days before had seemed so remote, something in the Far East, was upon us. Suddenly, we found ourselves on different continents, with the Atlantic Ocean between us.

Rattan
藤

Rattans are climbing palms from South East Asia, belonging to
the subfamily Calamoideae. Roots: from Malay rotan.

Of course, I often think of E's rattan chair. That chair symbolised our brief
passion. No one has sat on it since. Vacant. *Jadis, si je me souviens bien* . . .

The rattan chair was placed in the bedroom for obscure reasons: to
hang a wet towel after a bath, or to throw a pair of trousers on before
going to bed. I did not think anyone would normally sit on a chair in
a bedroom. It was redundant.

Once I asked him: Have you made love with other women on that
chair too?

He paused, and smiled strangely: Oh, that's a difficult question.

Only a while later, he told me that he never did. No, not on that
chair. In fact, he didn't even know where that chair came from. One day,
he just noticed that it had appeared in the apartment. It must have come
from someone who rented the apartment one summer. And now, it
is his chair. Our chair. Though I
am no longer there, and the chair
only belongs to my memory.

He sat in that chair holding
me. His entering hurt me slightly
at first. I gripped his shoulders.
His skin was sweaty on me as my
hips thrust.

II

Lexicon of Separations

6
Radical: 分

(separation, parting, disconnection)

Heaven is Boundless, Earth is Eternal
天长，地久

An expression from *Tao Te Ching*, attributed to Lao Tzu, from around 2,600 years ago.

Often, in the middle of the day, I would take the subway to Queens. I had no particular reason to bother myself with a long train ride across the city, apart from the desire to hear familiar tongues and eat familiar dishes.

One day, in Flushing's Chinatown, I walked into a Sichuan restaurant. I looked at a picture of lamb radish soup on the menu. My appetite rose. I realised that 'radish' has the same Latin root as 'radical', which is 'radix'. Yes, radish is a root vegetable. How coherent. Instantly I decided to order the dish. While I was waiting, I noticed a Chinese boy next to me humming a song. He had a pair of headphones on, absorbed in a tune that he could not help singing out loud. I recognised it:

天	长	地	久
sky	*tall*	*earth*	*old*

A more sophisticated translation could be: heaven is boundless, earth is eternal.

In Chinese, this expression has been overused, almost abused, in pop culture. It's a cliché. A serious Chinese writer would hesitate to use it to construct a literary work. But since I was in a foreign environment, my nostalgia for anything Chinese was aroused. Sky tall earth old. Where did this phrase come from? I started googling. What I found amazed me. It is originally from Lao Tzu's *Tao Te Ching*, 2,600 years ago.

But what is 天长地久 in its original context? One can safely assume it had nothing to do with romantic love, as it does in the song the boy was singing along to. Since *Tao Te Ching* was written in the ancient Chinese script, it's difficult to interpret the meaning.

天长地久。天地之所以能长且久者.
以其不自生也，故能长生。是以圣人后其身而身先.
外其身而身存，非以其无私邪？故能成其私。

Heaven is boundless, earth is eternal
Boundless and eternal
Because they do not exist for themselves
The sage steps back to be in front
Stays outside in order to remain within
Without self-interest and no self
He thereby realises his true nature.

My lamb radish soup arrived. Yes, I was still in the same place – a restaurant in Queens, in New York City. I had been time-travelling to the past, a misty and indeterminate landscape haunted by dragons and wandering sages. I looked at the dish. The lamb was braised with red chillies and green coriander. The radish was pink-red, sliced beautifully. The broth's hearty fragrance transported me back to my home town, and I felt homesickness simmer within me. Exactly what is *sky tall earth old*? Maybe it is food and nature. Fruit and salt. Or bounty of summer. Or the simple act of eating. As some Zen sage says: people think monkeys transporting themselves across the universe is a miracle; for me, the miracle is drinking tea and stirring the leaves.

I finished my soup, and headed back to Manhattan. On the subway, watching the passengers in and out of the carriage, I realised that I didn't have many days left before going back to Britain. I called E, I told him I would come straight to see him.

Self-pollinating
自我授粉

The pollination of a flower by pollen from the same plant.
Pollen: from Latin, 'fine powder'.

That was the beginning of our separation: an avocado, and the stone inside.

E had to leave me when it was time for me to pass through the security gate. JFK is not a nice place for such a memory. I imagined him sitting alone on the subway back to Manhattan, grim sights along that subway line, especially the part in Queens. But I was no longer involved in that sight, and that experience. My plane had left the skies over New York, and was now somewhere above the Atlantic. The flight would go on *forever*, I thought. I was despondent about our separation. Forever and hopeless – these were the words looping in my head.

The lights above the seats were turned off. We were supposed to sleep. I took out the avocado from my bag, and studied its label. It said that it was produced in Florida. Ah, an American product. I never told E that I had taken the avocado from his kitchen, from the fruit bowl kept by the sink. So that was the beginning of everything. I was eating an avocado on the way back across the ocean. I was thinking of E, and there were many ways of thinking of E. Eating an avocado from his kitchen was one of them.

With a small plastic knife I had found in an airport cafe, I peeled back the skin. Such a hard shell, like an animal's. The fibre inside was creamy. My fingers squeezed milky flesh out from the black skin.

Outside, total darkness and emptiness. I did not particularly want to know what was beneath me. Hopelessness was the ocean. We might be passing some islands. But there were no enchanted islands on this side of the world. I scraped out the last bit of soft flesh from the skin. Would anyone else on a plane eat an avocado as a snack, and eat it so slowly? Yes, perhaps a character in a postmodern novel.

Now all that was left in my palm was a large stone. It was beautiful, weighty and perfectly shaped. What to do with it? Maybe I should keep it. I should grow the seed. It would be easy to grow an avocado, since it is a self-pollinating plant. It would not need another avocado plant or butterflies or bees to help it to grow. Besides, there was a garden on the other side of the ocean, waiting for me and for this seed too.

Flyway

飞路

A flight path used in bird migration.

Birds migrate much more systematically than humans. When we migrate, or emigrate, we often act out of desperation. If there's a war or famine, we might try to escape and go anywhere better. Or we rush towards gold, blindly, from the east coast of China to the west coast of America.

But birds don't fly at random when they migrate, they follow a number of set roads. One of these is the East Atlantic Flyway. It stretches from Canada to Siberia, with wintering grounds in Western Europe and West Africa. Another is the Afro-Palearctic route which stretches from Europe and Asia to Africa. For many Arctic migrants, especially ducks, geese and swans, Western Europe is the final destination.

I will always remember the lines from the early pages of Salinger's *Catcher in the Rye*. The young boy speaks: '*I was thinking about the lagoon in Central Park, down near Central Park South. I was wondering if it would be frozen when I got home, and if it was, where did the ducks go.*'

Yes, where would the ducks in Central Park go when all is frozen? Such an innocent question. I wonder if Salinger knew that there is a type of migrant bird called a vagrant. Vagrants are the ones who are lost from the flock – often a young bird blown off course by storms. If it is lucky a vagrant might rejoin the flock on land or at sea, and find its flyway again. Perhaps the young hero – Holden Caulfield – is a vagrant.

What 'long distance' means for humans seems nothing compared with the distance travelled by migrant birds. A bird can fly for two hundred days straight without stopping. It will eat by catching whatever comes across its path in the air, and sleep while flying. Common swifts (楼燕) can fly for ten months without a break. That's three hundred days.

Right now, I am counting the days since I left America. Across the ocean, it's quite a distance. Perhaps I will read more about common swifts and their survival skills, I tell myself. But whenever I see J and our child playing in the back garden, my desire for long-distance flying diminishes. Still, I struggle to hold on to the idea.

Elective Affinities

选修亲和力

1809 novel by Johann Wolfgang von Goethe. The scientific term 'elective affinities' describes the tendency of chemical species to combine with certain substances in preference to others.

The Greek philosopher Empedocles said: 'People who love each other mix like water and wine; people who hate each other separate like water and oil'. This seems to be a perfect example of 'elective affinity'.

Goethe's *Elective Affinities* was the book E and I were both reading, though in different continents now. I bought the translation by David Constantine, and E bought the edition translated by Hollingdale. We had not been aware there were different translations. What a strange book to read, like a mirrored version of our life. Despite the fact that Goethe was a true polymath, I wondered how much he borrowed the idea from Empedocles. People who share similar values attract each other, otherwise they drive each other apart. Set near the German city Weimar, Eduard and Charlotte, an aristocratic couple, live an idyllic but slightly mundane life on a secluded garden estate; they decide to invite their friends, a man and a young woman, to live with them as Eduard's living experiment. I paused my reading and went back to read about Goethe.

Goethe wrote *Elective Affinities* when he was sixty. He must have drawn upon his experiences in Weimar, while living with his long-time lover Christiane Vulpius and their several children. This was a decade before he fell in love with a teenage girl, I noted. How strange, I thought, for a deep thinker and philosopher at the age of seventy-four after a near-fatal heart attack to fall in love with the young Ulrike von Levetzow. He even wanted to marry her. If Goethe were alive, would he still be respected, and worshipped as a human god?

Die Wahlverschaften is the German term for 'elective affinities', from *wahlen*, to choose, to elect, and *schaften*, properties. It is indeed ingenious to construct a novel about passion and companionship around a scientific concept. Somehow it also feels archetypically Germanic to me. It makes me wonder if chemical reactions between different elements are predetermined, and therefore fated. Fate is not a scientific term. But in Goethe's *Elective Affinities*, narrative and science seem to come together.

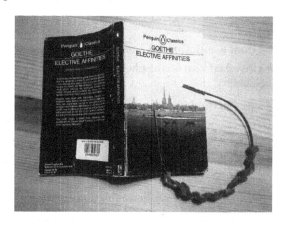

Heart

心

Old English heorte, Dutch hart, German Herz, French cœur,
Spanish corazón, Latin cor, cord-, Greek kēr, kardia.

Since parting from E and America, I often wrote to him with the same
question, or else asked him on the phone:

'How is your heart?'

He would pause, think for a few seconds, and say: 'I never know
how to answer that question.'

At other times, when I tried to end a conversation on the phone,
and to escape the quotidian topics, I would ask the same question.

And he would say: 'My heart? I will have a look.'

What is a heart? A heart is a hollow muscular organ that pumps the
blood through the circulatory system by contraction and dilation. It
has its symbolic function, because when a heart stops beating, one is
pronounced dead. Newborns have the fastest heartbeats. As we grow
older, the heart grows larger and heavier, therefore it beats slower
and slower.

When I was with E, the second month after we had met, I remember
lying against him and hearing his heart beat so fast. And I could see his
pulse through his thin shirt. I asked if he was feeling all right. He too
was concerned, and said he would go to the doctor. That afternoon, he
phoned me as he was leaving the clinic. He reported that the doctor
thought his heart rate was fine.

But still, why does it beat so fast? Should you worry about it? I
asked.

He gave no answer.

The French mathematician and writer Pascal said: 'The heart has its reasons, which reason does not know.' In Chinese, instead of saying 'I think', we say 'my heart thinks' – 我心想.

Scheidekünstler

化学分离家

The German verb 'scheiden' is used both for the chemical
process of separation and for 'sich scheiden lassen':'to get
a divorce.

I read much slower than E. I am not good at reading in my second language. But with Goethe's *Elective Affinities*, I read faster than usual. I was gripped by the book's plots as well as its literary experimentation.

In chapter 4, a man comes to live with the couple Eduard and Charlotte on their estate, and a discussion about elective affinities in chemistry is launched. Goethe's theory about chemical bonds is not too difficult to follow. He places it in the mouth of impassioned Eduard. It starts with two chemical elements, A and B, which have been in a harmonic state. Then C comes along. Supposing C attracts A, then B is *separated* from the unity with A. But the chemist will introduce a fourth element, D, then C will be bound to D. From there, Goethe writes about attraction and separation around his four characters.

Since E and I had been reading different translations, we compared our versions. In Constantine's translation, the protagonist Eduard refers to 'certain chemists who are skilled in the art of *separation* of substances' (*Scheidekünstler*). But in Hollingdale's version this becomes, 'a title of honour to chemists is to call them artists in *divorcing* one thing from another.'

Scheidekünstler is such an intriguing concept; the compound structure *Scheide* with *Künstler* makes this word totally unique. And one cannot translate it directly into English as 'a separation artist'. It sounds very wrong. A skilled chemist, perhaps? But that does not sound very interesting. Here we are, again, seeing the limitations of any given language.

Scheidung: divorce / 离婚
Trennung: separation / 分离

I lived a parallel life when I was in America. But after I returned to Britain, a different parallel life began. In London, my child and her father were in the same house as I was, but I talked to E in New York whenever I could.

Almost every day, we wrote to each other. But as was his way, E did not talk directly about us. He talked about Goethe's novel. As a fluent German speaker, he often mixed German words with English in his letters to me.

Scheidung was the word he used. But *Scheidung* means separation in legal terms. Since we were not married and perhaps would never do so, why did E use the word *Scheidung*? In German, to describe our separation would be *Trennung*, a much broader term. Thinking of our physical separation, these are the synonyms for parting: detachment, uncoupling, dissociation, disjunction, disunion, disaffiliation, segregation, partition, estrangement, and so on and so forth. We have successfully amassed a large number of words to express our (dis)connection.

Perhaps, if I want to make it more precise, our separation is *Trennung auf Zeit* – separation only for a limited time. Even though that limited time could be stretched, and it could even be infinite during our lifetime. Still, a lifetime is a limited period. We are no longer young. No wonder 'afterlife' is a perennial concept that is forever called upon.

Warfare

战争

Operations associated with conflict or battle. Hostilities.

My letters to E were getting longer, but E's responses to me were short, and often sparse. Perhaps I was caught in my inner monologue, and I was writing down everything on my mind without paying attention to his psychology. I realised that I was perhaps diminishing him by taking away his speech. What was I doing? We were separated by this ocean and by our own family commitments, but my heart seemed not to follow my mind, or to listen to reason. I wrote to E:

'How come I never hear you say "talk to me", or "I want to see you . . ."? You never demand anything from me. This feels unimaginable from my side as I need to talk to you every day (every hour if I can). You must be in some great level of self-control, or maybe love for you is not a "problem", a heartache, or a yearning. Is that because: 1. you are an Anglo-Saxon – surely this characteristic fact dominates your behaviour, 2. you are stable and balanced, 3. you are not so crazy about me, 4. you are a bit older and dampened by time. 5. I am an emotionally violent Third World person?'

And a few minutes later, perhaps more than ten minutes, or fifteen (it felt very long for me), I saw his response:

'It's definitely not 3, and I don't think it's 5. But your premise is wrong. If you want me to theatricalize my unhappiness, I can do so. It would go against 1. (an Anglo-Saxon never shows his suffering, which does not mean that he does not suffer). But I take note of what you ask here, and I think I know why you ask it. You have to stop with this kind of email. I'm not happy about having to constantly justify my behavior because it doesn't meet your expectations. Of course I want you to talk to me and I want to see you. I also want to deal with many other things. I hear what you say. Perhaps I'll be more explicit in saying what I am thinking, and tell you what I want from you.'

I read his email a few times, feeling hurt. I didn't write to him for a few hours. Then later, that night, I responded:

'On the contrary, I don't mean you should adjust your behaviour to suit me, I actually want to learn your quality and to live sanely. This quality of yours – being calm and being self-resourceful with situations like this, I don't know how to acquire that. It has eaten me every day – this need and yearning for love and communication – and at times, very often during certain hours of the day, it feels unbearable, other times I pretend I am okay and functioning in the passing of hours. If I have had a massive distraction, or multiple ones, then I might escape this daily suffering.'

Then I added:

'In the past, when I didn't want to be hurt, I told myself that I would be cold-hearted. I would never give myself totally to someone, so I would never feel lost. I need that but I forget how to do that. Perhaps I was never in love, not in such a way. Yes, I want to be sensible, to feel that I am an adult and I can cope with what's in front of me. Can you help me? Do I demand too much? Tonight when I was alone in the kitchen, preparing food – desolation came and swallowed me. I was in tears, but I didn't want to disturb you by calling you. A slave of love, how stupid I am.'

I don't know why I thought our communication had been 'drawn out', as one says of a war. But was it war between us? Certainly he was not my enemy. This hungry need for love was my enemy. Immature, childish, needy, rudimentary and, indeed, unsophisticated. The circumstance around us – the interruption in our physical love – was the enemy. Perhaps I ought to read Sun Tzu's *The Art of War* again. A well-known line from the book goes round my head: '*The supreme art of war is to subdue the enemy without fighting.*' But even Sun Tzu, I realised, could not help me.

7
Radical: 木

(wood, root, plant)

Divine Farmer

神農

The Divine Farmer – Shennong – is a mythological agricultural figure in ancient Chinese history. He is also called the God of Five Grains.

The Divine Farmer Shennong is thought to have taught the ancient Chinese not only the practice of agriculture – ploughshare, digging wells, seeding – but also the use of herbal medicines.

The Divine Farmer's Herb-Root Classic is an important manual from 2,000 years ago. In Chinese it is called *Bai Cao Jing* – a study of one hundred herbs. It is attributed to Shennong, but we don't really know its real author. It might have been written by a great agriculturist, or perhaps it was compiled by a group of herbalists and historians. No one knows.

The book records hundreds of herbal medicines and different types of plant, including a certain mushroom – 灵芝, *lingzhi*. I have always been fascinated by the description of this mushroom. I used to see *lingzhi* for sale in herbal shops when I was a child. We treated it as the most precious and miraculous of medicines. I was amazed by how large, thick and leathery the soft surface of a *lingzhi* was, even when it was totally dry. Later on, in my Western life, whenever I encountered some russet-coloured mushrooms in a forest, whether it was in southern Germany or in northern England, I always wondered if they might have been *lingzhi*, the magic cure for heart disease and high cholesterol. The Chinese name literally means divine fungus.

Shennong the Divine Farmer is one of the many Chinese gods we worship in temples. Even today, if you visit China, you encounter a large-scale Divine Farmer's Temple in every province. Peasants kneel in front of the statue with incense in their hands, praying for a bounteous harvest year.

Roots

根

From Old English rōt, and from Old Norse rót; related to Latin radix.

Some might find it baffling that I associate *The Divine Farmer's Herb-Root Classic* with *Lady Chatterley's Lover* by D. H. Lawrence. One is a Chinese herbal medicine guide, the other is a sensual romantic novel by an English author. But I don't see the disconnection here. 'Roots' is a solid earthy concept, at the same time totally metaphorical. Our body is the root of our emotional life, and our imagination.

Sexual passion can be found in every one of D. H. Lawrence's novels. In *Lady Chatterley's Lover*, or *Sons and Lovers*, love and sex permeate every page, and hold the meaning of the whole novel.

For Lawrence, the body is the root of life. To be rid of the needs of the body is to announce the death of life. In *A Propos of Lady Chatterley's Lover*, he wrote about how England has lost all sense of sensuality and feelings, to the extent that the English have come to be frightened by their own sexuality. In his words: '*Vitally, the human race is dying. It is like a great uprooted tree, with its roots in the air. We must plant ourselves again in the universe.*'

A great uprooted tree with its roots in the air – D. H. Lawrence announced that a hundred years ago. Is that how our civilisation looks today? In this century, we are gradually losing the traditional concept of 'home' or 'land', and we have gained more instant but virtual connection to the world, as well as thousands of choices in our minds (though not in our bodies yet). For Lawrence, mind and body cannot be divorced. In the same essay he expresses the idea that life is only bearable when the mind and the body are in harmony. The body is at best the tool of the mind, at worst, the toy. It feels to me that no other English author has expressed such an acute view on sensuality and on the loss of it.

In Chinese culture, 根 (roots) is a prominent metaphor and allegory. A major literary movement in the 1980s, after the traumatic Cultural Revolution, was called Back to Roots (寻根文学). 'Roots' in this context moves away from the Communist vocabulary which was produced after Mao's revolution, and returns to a more essential bodily expression. As a teenage poet, I was under the influence of this movement, rejecting ideological language but searching for a connection with nature, with our agricultural tradition. It is a tradition that came from the ancient times, rooted in the harmony between nature and human life. I was interested in writing about the beauty of the natural world. Morning dew on sugar cane plants, fishing boats under the moonlight, frogs in rice fields and newts on wet rocks, plum blossoms opening in the snow, farmers covered in mud returning home with their buffaloes at dusk, and essentially, myself, as a young woman, walking through landscapes and recording her experiences.

Flowers
花

In Middle English, 'flower' is sometimes written 'flour'. It is perhaps derived from Old French flour, flor.

In my personal lexicon, the word *flower* is as important as the word *root*. However poor and deprived my childhood might have been, I grew up in a southern landscape of flowers and trees. In those days, since Chinese people were still so reliant on agricultural knowledge, children would learn about the surrounding vegetation before they would learn how to read and write. In my case, from an early age, I could recognise different types of melons from looking at their flowers. I knew that small yellow flowers belonged to watermelons, large yellow prickly flowers belonged to winter melons, and fragrant ones belonged to honey melons. I knew how long to wait before the melon would ripen. I also remember how I got beaten up by a farmer. One day after school, I passed an orchard of pear trees and saw the beautiful white blossoms. I could not help taking two branches, each with six flowers. I did not realise the farmer was watching me. He was so furious that he chased me down the hill. Catching me, he beat me with his bare hands and shouted: 'Do you know I have lost twelve pears?! That's a lot of money!'

In those days, after the famine and Mao's Cultural Revolution, food was scarce. Twelve pears was a meal for twelve people.

In Samuel Johnson's dictionary, the definition for *flower* fills an entire page. Here is a tiny excerpt from Johnson's epic accumulation of associations:

The part of a plant which contains the seeds.

   Such are reckoned perfect flowers which have petals, a stamen, apex and stylus; and whatever flower wants either of these is imperfect. Perfect flowers are divided into simple ones, which are not composed of other smaller ones, and which usually have but one single style . . .

Imperfect flowers and *perfect* flowers? A curious idea. Johnson seems to have a creationist point of view about nature, as if there is an ideal and perfect nature. It makes one wonder about the concept of 'perfect man' and 'imperfect man'. What would be a perfect man for Johnson? What makes him think such a subjective definition would have any explanatory significance?

   'More than anything, I must have flowers always, always.' Claude Monet said this in his large garden estate in Normandy, in a village called Giverny. I have seen a few pictures of his house and garden as it is today. The house is large, with green wooden shutters on each window. In front are layers of red flowers. Perhaps they are poppies, or tulips, my eyes could not determine from the two-dimensional image. But there's a pond, with water lilies floating on the surface. Water lilies – *nymphéas.* Monet spent his last twenty years painting them, at sunrise, at sunset, in the rain, at night, again and again. He repeats and repeats, under endlessly varying conditions. This must have been an unending revising and attempting to re-see, just as the lilies or the tulips endlessly repeat the same patterns.

Azalea Walk
杜鹃花步道

A path in Central Park in New York, at West 76th Street, characterised by blooming azaleas and rhododendrons in springtime.

The azalea is not a common plant in England. But since I grew up with these pink and red flowering bushes that grow along the edges of bamboo forests, I miss seeing them. That's why today when I saw a blooming azalea plant in a local florist, I bought it. It was expensive, but not as costly as losing the connection with my past.

As I walked home with the little tree in my arms, I thought of Azalea Walk in Central Park. It was the beginning of spring, and I remember the walk E and I took near the Ramble and the Shakespeare Garden. I remember the azalea bushes looked dormant, though they had already sprouted young buds. We talked about the operas we wanted to see that weekend. There was a new production of *Madame Butterfly*, and I said I wanted to go. But we never went, nor did we ever see the azaleas bloom in the park.

Here in England, this azalea reminded me of my past. One flower but three different settings: the azaleas of my childhood in China, scattered here and there alongside the houses like fugitive children, neglected and wild; the azaleas of Central Park, pampered and self-important, but bloomless and dormant when I saw them; and the azaleas of England, somehow infinitely more exotic in this muted landscape of cloud and rain. All these differences, but the same floral nature. Like a neural link in my own brain, the flower spans many times and diverse places. I felt both my own inner separation, divided by my past experiences, and at the same time a unity, the mysterious continuity of life. As I sat contemplating, J ambled out of the kitchen and emptied some coffee grounds onto the bed of my newly acquired azalea.

The spell was broken.

Then J looked at me, holding the empty coffee pot, and asked: 'Are you missing New York?'

I nodded. J knew that I missed a certain person there. But gentle and attentive as he has always been, he didn't want to enter into the matter with me. We have separate minds therefore we are allowed to live in our separate thoughts. And that does not reduce the intimacy between us.

The Language of Flowers
花语

The structure and beauty of flowers is inexpressible in human
language, yet there is a language of flowers.

In one of the emails E wrote to me, he quoted lines from Georges
Bataille's *The Language of Flowers*. They explained that the structure
and beauty of flowers was inexpressible in human language, yet there
is a language of flowers. I wondered what this language of flowers was.

E and I wrote to each other about the state of the world, current
politics, the president of the USA, the prime minister of the UK, wea-
ther, nature, and plants especially. But we hardly talked about our
relationship, and whether we would visit each other when it was possible again. We became abstract lovers, a last step before all this would
become memory and past. In fact, we wrote to each other out of habit.
We could have written to our previous lovers or friends abroad, on a
regular basis. But we still wanted to grasp this thing between us even
if it was unattainable, like a hand reaching out to grasp the rushing
water in a river.

There is our human language about flowers, our narratives, our
projection of sentiment and feeling into these plants. But there is also
the natural 'language' of flowers which manifests itself independently of
human interpretation. It is the biological law that guides their growth
and death, and which goes beyond our capacities to describe, since
nature is inexhaustible. The structure of a flower is an expression of
nature. It shows reproductive organs, with stamens and carpels in the
centre, and brightly coloured petals and green sepals surrounding.

Then there's the cycle of a flower – bearing fruit and shedding seeds – this too is the language of nature.

Might Georges Bataille, in his fantastic prose, have been mixing these two senses of language? Bataille seemed to be more interested in the symbolic language of flowers. Just like many of us. If I see a red rose, I think of love. If I see a white chrysanthemum, I think of death. We are hopelessly limited. We merely want nature to be our life's textbook, coded with meanings. We live in our own narrative, a closed circle, as E might say.

Flowers speak to everyone. But then there are the flowers that speak only to you in a specific way. My azaleas seem to contain a special meaning, woven into them, for me, that other people cannot perceive.

Daisy

雏菊

Old English dæges ēage 'day's eye', perhaps it's because the flower opens in the morning and closes at night.

It's the season of daisies. On Sunday I bought another white margarita from Columbia Road Flower Market. I planted it next to the azalea.

Daisies are less dramatic than azaleas. In Chinese culture, azaleas are *si xiang shu*: homesick trees. They are the symbol of nostalgia and homesickness. But daisies, as far as I can remember, are used only as herbal medicines in China. Dried daisies can be boiled in tea and they can reduce inflammation and cool your body's inner heat. Here in the West, the flower seems to be associated with an ambiguity of love and sexuality. A song from Shakespeare's *Love's Labour's Lost* contains the lines:

When daisies pied and violets blue,
And lady-smocks all silver-white
And cuckoo-buds of yellow hue
Do paint the meadows with delight,
The cuckoo then, on every tree,
Mocks married men; for thus sings he:
'Cuckoo; Cuckoo, cuckoo!'

'Pied' – multicoloured, or a two-coloured thing like a black-and-white magpie. And 'pied beauty' implies disloyalty. The song is about wives cheating on their husbands, as the reference to the cuckoo mocking married men hints at.

But isn't Shakespeare being moralistic? There are barely any innocent flowers in his poetry. Here, I prefer the game that young girls play in the spring fields. 'He loves me, he loves me not,' sings a girl, picking up a daisy from the meadow and pulling off each petal as she holds the little blossom. What does it mean, this 'he loves me, he loves me not' ritual? Does it suggest we ought to leave it to nature to decide fate? The flower will know the answer, not us.

I am fond of these small flowers. They are simple, humble, and happy in little pots in my garden. Every day, as I wake up and go down to the garden to check them, their petals are open. They bloom in such a discreet manner, through rain and sun.

Florimania
花痴

Latin flōs, flōr-, for flower; and -mania for madness.

As I had left America, I didn't know if I needed to tell E how obsessive I am, because I guess it didn't matter any more. But I am totally obsessive, especially as a gardener. I can't say that I wouldn't abandon art if I had a large and luscious garden. The first thing I do in the morning, after waking, is to go out into the garden and observe any changes in my plants. They might have grown slightly taller, or a new shoot might have emerged during the night, or a young bud might be about to open. And I sweep leaves from the ground with a broom so that I can walk in my bare feet. I impatiently fill a bucket with water, as if the plants might die if the water arrives one minute late. I become crazy if I find a dead branch or some uninteresting weeds invading a flowerpot. Or if I discover a slug hiding under a cucumber leaf, or aphids plaguing new roses. I stare at the problematic plants and diagnose them and find solutions. Sometimes I have no solution. For example, once a mimosa tree refused to grow vertically – it spread horizontally, taking over my tiny garden. Painfully I chopped the horizontal branches, hoping that the main branch would gain strength and stretch up into the sky against gravity.

The nature of my florimania is primitive, almost biological. There is nothing so grand about it. It's just that I want to embody a human life with plants. A life without plants is a life without heart.

Euphoria
幸福的

Euphoria derives from the Greek euphoros, meaning 'healthy'.
It was originally a medical term in its English use, meaning a
feeling of well-being.

After E and I had been apart for some months, he mentioned in one
of his emails that the brief days we passed together were a kind of
'euphoria'. I know something about happiness, and joy, even bliss. But
euphoria? It is not a word I would normally use. And I don't remember
him ever using that word with me when we were together.

Most dictionaries tell me the feeling of euphoria is characterised by
intense excitement and happiness.

When we were still physically together, my body was often hungry
for him. But his body didn't always work. His body was frozen sometimes. Then, when his body was awake, I would receive him. I was in
a *euphoric* state. So that was the word – it came naturally, only then,
and only as an adjective. For me, adjectives describe a more temporary
state, unlike nouns. I loved it when he continued to touch me after I'd
had an orgasm. I felt an intensely warm pleasure while my body was
still trembling.

To me, a non-native English speaker, the word 'euphoria' sounds
like something else. It reminds me of the name of a very special evergreen plant – euphorbia. The colour of the flowers is the colour of the
leaves: green. One of my favourite shrubs, it blends into the wilderness,
becoming almost invisible. Its common name is wood spurge. I have

never grown it in my garden. But I always love looking at them when I encounter these bushy blossoms in the park, or by the roadside.

Euphoria – E, my grief. Euphorbia – evergreen flowers.

Browsing / Grazing
采叶 / 牧草

The two ways animals feed themselves in nature.

I am not a goat, because goats are browsers. Browsing is foraging on the upper layers of vegetation. With grazing, animals, such as sheep, feed on grass or other low-lying plants. Therefore I am a sheep.

I am a humble sheep, but not as humble as a deer. Apparently, deer love to browse thorny plants, such as roses or hawthorn. How strange. Doesn't a little deer get hurt by the thorns? We poor humans can barely suffer a sting or a graze. The idea of supping on thorny bushes is inconceivable. How did *Homo sapiens* become so soft and permeable? We are animals, but with barely any bodily defence. All we have is cunning.

When I was very young, my father used to say that his big son, my brother, would eat the top layer of the shoots, which is tender and fresh, while his young daughter, me, would eat what was left underneath. I had been foraging around, after leaving China for the West. When my father died, my brother still lived in the home town where we had grown up, whereas I kept escaping, moving farther and farther away to forage. Two years after I arrived in England, I decided to move to France, because I had felt very disorientated in London. But life in Paris was acidly lonely. I did not manage to put down roots, or even have my own patch of grass. Again, drifting around, I ventured next to Germany, then moved back to England. And a decade later, America. Because I thought I needed a new continent, and the grass would be greener there. And now, it seems that I have returned, to where I should be, where I can more or less recognise the vegetation at my feet. Am I still grazing the bottom part of a plant? Or have I managed to learn to both graze and browse?

Camellia

茶花

Named by Carl Linnaeus after Joseph Kamel, a seventeenth-century Moravian botanist.

I have grown three camellia plants since I returned to London. Two with red blossoms, one with white. My garden has a different shape now. J has not noticed the existence of these particular plants, and he almost never does. My child knows the camellia, because I repeatedly tell her about plants in our garden, or out in the park.

The camellias transport me back to the Met Opera House at Lincoln Center. It was my first time doing something quite formal and – can I say? – bourgeois with E. I confess that I have never been interested in opera, not even Verdi, not even *La Traviata*. For sure, I am from peasant stock, and this classical form has always felt heavy to me.

La traviata means 'the woman who strayed'. The common translation is 'the fallen woman'.

We were seated early. Gradually the audience came in, filling the hall, the aisles and the balconies. For a long time we stared at the stage curtain. It was possibly the most beautiful thing from that night. It was a projection of an enormous white camellia onto a deep blue background. So exquisite, I would have been happy if we had just watched this all night. But the curtain was finally raised, and the opera started. Violette, the Fallen Woman, appeared. She stood in a white dress on a stage decorated with white flowers.

Flowers everywhere, as far as my eyes could see. Were all these camellias?

I read somewhere that Verdi had a large garden estate in Sant'Agata, in northern Italy. And he was a great gardener too. Apparently, every time he finished composing an opera, he would grow a tree on his land. At one point in his life, he gave up opera and spent three years gardening. After these three years he returned to music and wrote *Aida*. Did the great composer know that camellias originated in China? And that they are related to prized tea plants that the Europeans, for centuries, tried desperately to obtain? Perhaps Verdi knew it well, as the two Opium Wars occurred during his lifetime. But maybe he did not care about the wars, or the origin of his plants. He had lost his wife and his two children in the early years of his marriage. He had become an atheist in the meantime. He needed no external war to distract him. Operas and trees were his redemption.

Almost all love stories are autobiographical. The writer Alexandre Dumas *fils* spent only a year with his lover – a young courtesan named Marie Duplessis, the inspiration for Violette. Perhaps Dumas' father persuaded him to leave the girl, just like in the novel. Or his mistress moved on – she is believed to have become the mistress of the composer Franz Liszt. But at least Dumas managed to write *La Dame aux Camélias*, the tragic love story on which *La Traviata* is based.

When Marie Duplessis died of tuberculosis, she was only twenty-three. She was buried in Montmartre Cemetery in 1847. I wonder what inscription is engraved on her headstone, or if it is covered over with moss. Or has it been erased, after almost two hundred years of rain, sun and ice?

8

Radical: 疒

(malady, disease, disorder)

Flu (Influenza)
流感

From medieval Latin influentia via Italian, literally 'influence'.

The Chinese word 流感 (*liu gan*) literally means *floating feeling*. Which sounds strange in English, but *gan* – feeling – means many things in Chinese, including sensations, such as cold. A floating cold is the flu.

According to the Swedish film-maker Ingmar Bergman, making films is like catching the flu. Bergman is well known for *The Seventh Seal* and *Wild Strawberries* from the 1950s. In an interview for ITV's *The South Bank Show* in 1978, Bergman told Melvyn Bragg he felt the 'flu effect' after making *Scenes from a Marriage*. Flu? Melvyn Bragg repeated the word in some confusion. 'Yes, flu, like the virus. You must have this virus! So that it can infect your actors, infect your film team with what you have in your body!' the master declaimed, in his powerful and affirmative way of speaking.

Endemic + Pandemic
地方病 + 流行病

From Greek, en, pan + dēmos 'people'.

'Pandemic' comes from the Greek, from the root word *dēmos*, 'people', and the prefix *pan* meaning 'all'. 'Pandemic' has much greater cognitive force than the lesser-used term 'endemic'. The prefix *en* means 'in'. Endemic does not conjure up images of deserted streets and mass graves, whereas pandemic does.

It's at the edges of the human empire that pandemics begin. They start on the borders of human settlement and nature. They start with human encroachment. When bats or pangolins have no forests to move about in any more, they hide on the urban outskirts. Or they try to live in dumping grounds of human waste. This forced intimacy between wild animals and our urban space is a hostile relationship. We are killing each other. Viruses are transmitted from one body to the other, mutation happens without our knowing. Backyard poultry production in Asia has been linked to bird flu, eating bushmeat in parts of Africa with Ebola and HIV, close contact with a certain species of pig in Mexico with swine flu.

The animal hosts carrying the viruses are biological foreigners we invite unwittingly into our enclosure. We use their body parts, treat them as commodities and curiosities. Their fur and scales, horns and claws fascinate us. We attribute to them symbolic and curative powers. We sup on their inner organs as delicacies. We think we are in control, but a silent intimacy links our bodies to theirs, and the mutated viral forms permeate our skin.

As I think of this silent intimacy, I think of E. This pandemic is part of our story, although exactly how I can see only dimly, confusedly. We had felt this intimacy surrounding us, even when we first met. It was a dangerous feeling, as we both sensed that we should not enter its realm. Was our attraction a portent of a mutually dangerous infectious event which would sweep us up? We both knew that it was growing even before our bodies engaged. Then we were torn apart by the pandemic, separated by a suddenly untraversable ocean. But to be a human means to be a living organism vulnerable to intrusion. Perhaps we are destined to be inhabited by bodies and lives foreign to us. To E, my body represented a foreign intrusion, at least in the beginning of our story. His first reaction was to withdraw, to evade being invaded. Or perhaps that was just the dance we performed. But very quickly he inhabited me, and our worlds merged.

Pangolin
穿山甲

From Malay peng-guling. An old-world mammal with a body covered in scales. It's also called tenggiling, and trenggiling. Swedish zoologist Carl Linnaeus invented the neo-Latin genus name *Manis* for pangolins in the eighteenth century.

Pangolins are the most trafficked mammals in the world today. A strange but endearing creature, it looks like a reptile but is a mammal, and it appears to be a cross between a poodle and a dragon. It can coil up into a ball (known as volvation). It licks ants from shrubs, and it is nocturnal.

It has always been present in Chinese mythology. Its Chinese name 穿山甲 means, literally, cross mountain metal.

Some Chinese people believe that the animal can cure maladies such as fever, anxiety, fear, and also children's illnesses. What is the origin of these beliefs? Magical beliefs are based on resemblances. The rhino's horn looks like an erection; the tiger is strong, so eating its penis might give you potency; the wetness of the oyster's flesh suggests sexual readiness; and the turtle's shell demonstrates the substance of a long life. This magical thinking sees the world as an interconnected web of resemblances, of sympathies and antipathies. The microcosm reflects the macrocosm. Foucault wrote in *The Order of Things* that in medieval times, humans tried to find resemblances between our society and the natural world, between our body and the cosmos, and this medieval practice has continued today, in China and in many other traditional societies. It's a world view that does not really fit with modern science, and perhaps some day these poetic or spiritual beliefs will be stripped away. Indeed, we humans are both the comedy and tragedy spun from our own vivid imaginations.

Hellblau
浅蓝

German, light blue (hell: bright and light; blau: blue)

I had been back in London for some months. My mind still shifted between two cities. Sometimes when I was talking to J at home, it was as though I was talking to E in his New York apartment. Then I realised the different faces, the different settings. In our recent correspondence, E and I agreed that we should not talk about love. This separation is too long to bear; the best *solution* would be just to stop writing to each other altogether. Solution – was this the word we both used? What a horrible word. It left me in anguish, though we know it had been nothing but anguish since we parted.

I suppressed my feelings. I didn't want to carry the image of E in my head, nor his voice. Leaving the house in the early morning, I went for a run. But running in a chilly English wind didn't soothe me. I was still caught in my inner monologue. Twenty minutes later I found myself returning home, shivering.

My body had been in pain for the last few days, and it would continue to ache until my period arrived. Always around the pelvis. Always to do with a woman's reproductive system. But maybe the pain had to do with something else. How do you tell a man that you are in physical pain, when there is no diagnosis? In the Western world, all pains have medical terms and they come with explanations and possible solutions, yes *solutions*, even though some might be incurable.

I thought of all this, and wanted to write to E about it. But I should not. Romance is a disturbing state, especially when the couple are no longer physically together. So why was I still writing to him with such desperation? I wondered if there was such a thing as Third World emotion. A person whose feelings and behaviour have been shaped by an abusive past and poverty in early life. I had endured that abuse and biting poverty for half of my life. I now know that my emotions come from that. And at the same time, as a woman from the Third World (the China I grew up in, not the First World China of today), I have this almost automatic surrender to a cultured man of the First World. I surrender but at the same time I reclaim my lost rights. Give it to me, give it back, I hear a child crying and screaming in my stomach.

A sudden throbbing pain in my right thigh. My hips hurt . . . I must lie on the sofa. Tears came, all of sudden.

I meditated. Time passed. Motionless and soundless. Almost like death. But my tears dried out, at least. During my meditation, images of E, his apartment, his bedroom with the shutters closed, his solitary rattan chair by the window, his small kitchen, his office, and the way he swung his arms while he walked occupied my mind. It was a struggle to empty them out.

We didn't communicate that day. Later that night, in a text message, E asked me to use a word to describe my feeling. Just a word, he said. What can I answer? Fine, or not fine, neither could explain my need and my lack. I am a woman trapped by domesticity and family duty. But I won't show that, I won't tell anyone about it. So I turned inwards. I turned to myself, to meditate, to dilute, and to disappear. Sending him one word might satisfy his need to know I am still responding to him. A sign of ordinary struggle, every day, alone and inwards. A normality. But so what? Does he really need to know that? Or is it just some code of good conduct? All this time I have told him that he is dealing with a woman with multiple lives and desires and troubles, *one word* is no way to describe this woman, this me, and this situation.

I thought more about his message. And I thought of the word he might want to hear. What about an equivocal word to respond to his question?

Hellblau. Light blue.

He said our relationship now is built on nothing but words. *Hellblau* is one of those words, like other pleasing or poetic words we use in our writing. But what I have been writing to him, and what I have spoken to him, are not *just* words. My words are never just words. They are my very physical existence. They are the lexicon of my realities.

Who's Afraid of the Big Bad Wolf?
谁怕大灰狼

A song written by Frank Churchill featured in the 1933 Disney cartoon *Three Little Pigs*.

That was our last hedonistic night before our separation. I had seen only the film version of *Who's Afraid of Virginia Woolf?*, with Elizabeth Taylor, but it was years ago and all I could recall was the constant shouting between the husband and the wife. Perhaps I had been too young to understand it. I was not into the idea of 'the couple', nor domestic battles. But this new production of the play would teach me everything about couple culture, or something deeper and larger, I believed.

The set, a large carpeted living room with armchairs, sofas and bookshelves, was realistic, almost too realistic. Bombarded by the cries and screams between the man and the woman, we were disturbed throughout the play. During the interval, I felt slightly paralysed, unable to get up from my seat. And what about the audience that night? I hesitated to point out to E that most of them were middle-aged and well dressed. I was one of the few younger ones. Theatre and marriage. Only old wealthy couples can afford to see a staged marriage story.

We walked out of the theatre, looking for a bar where we could sit and reflect. The lines between Martha and George rang in my ears:

Martha: Truth or illusion, George; you don't know the difference.
George: No, but we must carry on as though we did.
Martha: Amen.

The song too rang in my ears as we descended into the soft wind of the early-spring night. Who's afraid of the big bad wolf, the big bad wolf, the big bad wolf? Who's afraid of the big bad wolf? We didn't give a single thought to the outside world. The big bad wolf belongs to a story, not to a reality.

Unoccupied

无人居住

From Latin occupare, 'seize'.

A photo of Times Square one evening during the pandemic, in the *New York Times*. The great emptiness. All the neon lights are still lit, but the streets are devoid of humans. It's so clean and unoccupied. It is almost beautiful. And I remember our night-time outings looking for theatres and bars among multitudes of people. The crowds flowed in and out of theatres and cinemas, creating ceaseless human waves. It is hard to believe that Times Square could be empty, without a single soul. I had to admit that the unoccupied square captured in that photo looked more mysterious than the occupied one. How long can these neon lights last without human interference? If they were to go off one day, all of them, would that be the end of New York, the end, even, of American entertainment culture? Lyceum Theatre, Booth, Palace, Al Hirschfeld Theatre . . . That night in March was our last night, before I flew back to London. We didn't know the virus would hit the world so badly. We just worried about our imminent separation. Nothing that happened that day could fade from my memory. In the dusk we took the subway to 42nd Street. Everything was normal; the pandemic still hadn't become our reality. My hand in E's. Often he took his hand back to check the time. When we got to 45th Street, we saw the huge posters for *Who's Afraid of Virginia Woolf?* There was a queue for return tickets. We had polite exchanges with a doorman as well as a cashier while picking up our tickets. A week later, we learned the doorman had the virus, or the cashier, or the usher, I don't know exactly. But that night, we were possessed by something else. Something to do with passion and consumption.

They say that in times of war people organise huge parties and exuberant celebrations, even though they might die the next day. Perhaps unwittingly E and I were experiencing something similar, on a different scale, but suffering from the same syndrome.

9

Radical: 走

(walk, step, move)

Bicycle
自行车

From bi- 'two' + Greek kuklos 'wheel'.

For some years (not every day, but from time to time), I thought about Beckett's *Molloy*. There is one particular line: *It was like being in China.* The line seems to be casually placed in Beckett's stream of consciousness, but it always struck me whenever I reread the passage:

> *Let me cry out then, it's said to be good for you. Yes, let me cry out, this time, then another time perhaps, then perhaps a last time. Cry out that the declining sun fell full on the white wall of the barracks. It was like being in China. A confused shadow was cast. It was I and my bicycle.*

The novel is about a man who spends much of his time on his bicycle as he moves about in some anonymous countryside, encountering people. There is no story, no recognisable location, just a restless and maddening voice. I could never grasp the meaning of the book. Perhaps I am blocked by its linguistic barrier, a style that belonged only to Beckett. The writing is difficult for a non-native European like me. Besides, Beckett wrote it in French first. But what puzzles me is not the book itself, it is that line: *It was like being in China.* Each time I read it I wonder endlessly about what Beckett meant. The author had never been to China. He wrote it around 1951, after his experience in the French Resistance under German occupation. But the most famous Asian bicycle – Flying Pigeon – was mass-produced in China under Mao's command in 1950. Already back then bicycles were integrated into city planning. I am curious about how Westerners perceive China and its bicycles without witnessing the actuality in person. Maybe that is obvious.

Bicycles in China were already popular in the mid nineteenth century. In the twentieth century it was normal that a poor Chinese man could not have a wife but he would have a bicycle. It was like owning a buffalo in the old days. And perhaps the phenomenon was widespread in the whole of East Asia. A notorious event during World War II was when the Japanese Army rode down from the Malay Peninsula into Singapore and captured British soldiers. It was a big embarrassment for the British Empire – losing Singapore to a bunch of little Asians on their little bicycles!

But maybe I am completely wrong. Maybe Beckett's line has nothing to do with his perception of China and bicycles. The shadow cast by Molloy and his bicycle on the white wall of the barracks looks to Molloy like a Chinese hieroglyph. Yes, a hieroglyph; a man looks like a man, a two-wheeled cart looks like a two-wheeled cart. Here is the Chinese character for this two-wheeled thing: 车 – *che*, and it has been evolved and shape-shifting for the last 3,000 years.

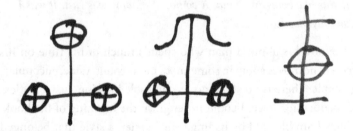

Plain / Fade
平淡

A word used in Roland Barthes's essay on 1960s China.

Roland Barthes, on his way back from Japan to Europe, stopped in Beijing. It was the 1960s, and he didn't understand that the vast country was going through the turmoil of the Cultural Revolution. He stood in front of grey-jacketed workers on their rustic black bikes. He thought, what a plain and grey country China was. 'Plain' is the word he used, or rather, his original French, *fade*. He himself was not even sure it was the right adjective to describe his impressions of the factories, the schools and the cities he saw. He then switched to a different word, *paisible* (peaceable). He wrote them in his notebook, which was published later in *Le Monde*.

Plain (or *fade*) and peaceful (or *paisible*) are very different concepts. Surely *paisible* was not the right word to describe a country filled with labour camps. But maybe *fade* has some truth to it: everyone wore grey or blue uniforms and Beijing was a smoggy industrial city. All the old 'feudal' scenes such as temples or operas or tea houses could not be exposed to foreigners, due to their counter-revolutionary nature.

Unlike many from that time, such as Sartre, Beauvoir, Pasolini and Godard, who were fascinated by Mao and Communism, Barthes was not interested in China at all. He was always off-centre. Beijing then was a very strange place on this planet. Or should I say *Peking*, according to the common Western pronunciation, a mimicking of what Chinese people might have uttered in relation to their capital? (Indeed, an onomatopoeia.) Barthes didn't come to Beijing looking for the empire of signs, nor did he stop in China to compare the workers' food to the exquisite dishes of Japan. Did he stop by in the hope of maybe finally tracing the origins of ideograms? He didn't find anything in the end. And that's not what a semiologist is supposed to find anyway. Nor did he find eroticism – as he remarked in his notebook, 'absence of eroticism' was part of the plainness of China then. In Communist China, the word for plain is 朴素 – *pu su*. It means humble, modest and unpretentious. It is a political word, very popular in the 1960s and 70s. I wonder how long it will last, if a word too has its own lifespan, like us humans.

And Chinese society is no longer very *pu su*. If anything, it is the opposite now.

Automobile

汽车

The Chinese word for automobile is qi che, 'steam cart', and it has never been replaced by a more appropriate term.

I have never owned a car, nor have I ever passed my driving test. This explains why I have always lived in big cities with convenient public transport. A long time ago, when I graduated from university, I did try to learn to drive. But the military style of that driving school outside Beijing (in Changping, an industrial suburb) killed my desire to embrace the motorways. Even though I appreciate highways, which take me speedily from my house to an airport, I always dread looking out onto the grim grey concrete, and even after all these years my carsickness has never improved. It must be some sort of anti-modernity syndrome.

I have always loved the work of Swiss dramatist Friedrich Dürrenmatt. One of his philosophical essays is entitled 'Automobile and Railroad Nations'. It is a wonderful meditation on the relation between political systems and modernity. Two hundred years ago Switzerland was an enclosed mountain region, even though it was the crossroads of Europe. It must have undergone immense transformations as the railways, tunnels and motorways were being built. Dürrenmatt responded to this radical transition in relation to the old Swiss landscape. In 'Automobile and Railroad Nations', the author's position against modern political systems is clear:

In the beginning, this happy pedestrian society enjoyed unlimited freedom; everyone left his house whenever he wanted and wandered off wherever he wished; not even roads were needed, footpaths were sufficient; to bridge a stream, a tree was cut down, and where a river could not be forded, ropes were strung tightly from bank to bank.

Such a view is of course an illusion. Humans always need to make roads and to build bridges; even bush people and aboriginals need to cut down their jungle to make paths. 'Unlimited freedom' also suggests unlimited danger. But from a nostalgic point of view, I wholeheartedly feel the old Swiss man's sentiment. I will always remember a scene I witnessed from a car during one of my visits to my home town after I had left China. On a brand-new highway leading to a newly built airport, an old farmer was trying to cross the barrier of the highway with his two buffaloes. He was beating his animals hard with a stick, but the animals would not raise their forelegs. They stayed by the barrier, stubbornly lost. Such a sorrowful scene . . . And what did I do? I let the car take me away, as fast as it could, to the airport which would take me even further away from that scene. I, a daughter of that very agricultural tradition, have fully embraced the modernity of this Western society. The only gesture I could make is as senseless as that of the buffalo, producing wistful words at the edge of monolithic cities.

Peony

牡丹

From Greek paiōnia, from Paiōn, the name of the physician of the gods.

I wrote to E about the blossoming peony in my garden. I asked if he ever went back to the Botanic Garden in the Bronx. When we were there, we saw some magnificent peonies, along with equally magnificent orchids. At first, E thought they were roses, but I explained that roses come with thorns. The peony has no thorns, and has a large flower head.

Peony flowers can be pink, white or red. Their blooms are large and showy with elaborate folds. According to Greek myth, the peony is named after Paeon, a student of Asclepius, the god of medicine and healing. In mythology, Paeon is such a talented student that Asclepius becomes jealous of his pupil and tries to punish him. But Zeus saves Paeon from the wrath of Asclepius by turning him into a peony flower.

A man becomes a flower. That's an interesting reincarnation.

In China, 牡丹 – *mu dan* – is one of the most beloved native flowers. They were particularly popular during the Tang Dynasty as they were grown in the imperial gardens. In the tenth century the cultivation of peonies spread throughout China, and the seat of the Sung Dynasty, Luoyang, was the centre of its cultivation.

I had never been to Luoyang, the legendary flower capital. Nor had I been to the province – Henan – in the central plain of China. Now that it seemed I was becoming a Westerner, I wondered if I would ever visit that area, the birthplace of Chinese civilisation. I felt I had done all my long-distance travelling. At this moment my life was centred around my house. In between tending my garden and looking after my child, I sat by the desk and reflected like an old man in his final days. I asked myself: What really matters in my life at this stage, after all these encounters? Of course, I answered, there was surviving! But beyond that, what was there that mattered? An equation came to me: life = home + art + plants? Then another: life = family + health + gardening? I was surprised that artistic practices didn't weigh much in these calculations. I was not like the gifted medical student Paeon, so talented he was punished by his teacher Asclepius by being reduced to a flower rooted in the soil. But still, a flower has its aesthetic value, I thought to myself. A life without beauty is unbearable. Perhaps, a *Lebenskünstlerin* – a life artist – was the answer to these questions that bothered me.

Immobility
不动

From Latin: in- 'not' + mobilis 'move'.

Now that I think about it, why does Zeus save Paeon – the physician of the gods – from Asclepius, by turning him into a peony? Is it a good thing to be a flower? Especially a flower like a peony? Even the greatest flowers are immobile. Even a five-metre-tall happily growing bamboo is immobile. Even a gigantic ancient banyan tree with hundreds of roots spreading over the ground is immobile.

But every plant is like the dandelion – its body parts scatter in the wind and land far and wide. And every fruit – a gooseberry, a tomato, a hazelnut – will be eaten by a bird, or a little animal, and its seeds will grow wherever they are dropped. The regeneration of plants perhaps is not that different from that of humans. I thought about this several years ago when I decided to give birth to my child and to bring her up in Britain with J. This was a way to continue my life. Even though I did not consciously think that I was regenerating my life through my reproductive system. But here I was, nature took its decision, and my giving birth led me to a new state, one of feminine immobility as a mother. Like the plant rooted in the soil, whose fruits and flowers are scattered about, I was rooted in domesticity, my child moving about me, and readying herself to be cast into the world.

Wu Wei

无为

A Taoist concept from the ancient philosopher Lao Tzu: wu wei – actions without acting, doings by non-doing. What it really means is effortless action, free-flowing spontaneity.

Britain now, for me, was about being stuck. I was in the same spot treading water. The pandemic had radically changed ways of living and working and travelling. Child, school, house, work. The domestic was like a heavy treacle I could not move my limbs through. Maybe I should release myself. I should think of Lao Tzu, and the concept of *wu wei*.

Lao Tzu (literally Old Master), the author of *Tao Te Ching*, is a mythical figure. We can never be sure if he was real, since little is known about his actual life. And being Chinese doesn't help; it does not give me any special authority or access to more facts about Lao Tzu. No one knows the years of his birth or death. Not that these dates are crucial to define a man's existence. Who could truly imagine the facial details and physical presence of a man who lived 2,600 years ago? Let alone pin these details down with words? The only thing we know about him is that he was a scholar and archivist for the royal court of Zhou. The only images relating to this laughing saint are various paintings of him riding a water buffalo. For some reason, he is always on the back of a buffalo. Why is he not on the back of a donkey, or a horse?

According to Chinese legend, in his later years Lao Tzu grew weary of the moral decline in the country, and decided to leave society behind by disappearing. This makes me think of another grand old man's departure, 2,000 years later. One winter night, Tolstoy left his house on foot and vanished. Some days later, he was found dead by a train station. Perhaps Lao Tzu didn't die such a mysterious or tragic death. His death remains unknown to the world. A *wu wei* death, a spontaneity. Ashes to ashes, dust to dust, it's the death of a true Taoist. Light, improvised and organic, just like the traceless dying and decomposition of an ancient buffalo.

Yes, *wu wei*. Do not act. This is something I ought to embody since my return to Britain. *Wu wei* is the only principle to keep my current life in order.

Zheng He's Navigation Maps
郑和航海图

Also called Mao Kun Map, and including some Stella Charts, these maps were produced by the great explorer Zheng He from his seven voyages during the fifteenth century.

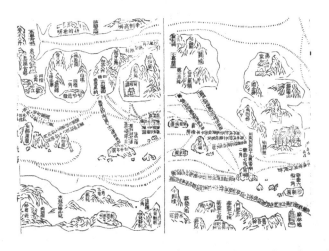

I dreamt of travelling. But the pandemic made travel undesirable. When I am stuck in a physical place, I look at maps, especially ancient maps. Apparently, that's what people used to do in the days when travel was a luxury for the few, maybe only a fantasy for the rest. One day, I found myself standing in front of the King George III map collections at the British Library. I looked at the old maritime maps, housed in glass cases, illuminated by dim spotlights. I also looked at the visitors in the hall. They were older, and a few were in wheelchairs, all of us looking at symbols of adventure and distant journeys.

I wandered about in front of European atlases, globes and ancient Indian maps. But I wanted to find some Chinese maps. I saw a few, but I could not find the only ancient Chinese maps I really know, which I first learned about at school. It was Zheng He's Navigation Maps, and I remember when I was young I was struck by its waving drawings of landscape and sea.

Zheng He, a Muslim eunuch from the fifteenth century, was the captain who led the treasure fleets of the Ming Dynasty on world voyages. Zheng's fleets visited Java, Thailand, South East Asia, India, the Horn of Africa, Arabia and Australia. In each of his seven voyages, Zheng He presented gifts of gold, silver, porcelain and silk; in return, Ming China received 'exotic' creatures such as ostriches, zebras and camels, and ivory from the Swahili coast. Apparently, Zheng brought back a giraffe from Kenya. In the Ming court, they worshipped this strange creature, and treated it as an animal from heaven. The Chinese name for giraffe is *changjinglu* – 'long-necked-deer' – and I wonder if the name might have come from that time, when Zheng He presented the animal to the Ming emperor.

Zheng He's maps are sophisticated and childlike at the same time. Mountains and water are detailed with ink-brush, along with strange names assigned to different lands. In these mesmerising drawings, you cannot find a trace of appropriation, or the act of renaming a place, but a respect for the bounty of foreign hills and strange seas. Somehow these hand-drawn pictures demonstrate that we humans are only the temporary passengers of the known and unknown landscape.

Zheng died at sea during his last voyage. The Chinese emperors dropped their interest in overseas affairs and China returned to self-absorption and isolation. But that's not the end of the story. There are tantalising suggestions that Zheng's maps of the explored territories made their way into the hands of European explorers, even into the hands of Christopher Columbus. Was Columbus guided by these luminous depictions of ocean, land and sky? We do not know. But our geography teachers in our Chinese schools certainly believed so.

10

Radical: 身

(body, flesh, figure)

Morpheus
孟菲斯

Morpheus is the Greek god of form or shape. In Ovid's poem, he
is the son of sleep.

Another month passed. Days were so much longer. With the changing
light, J became an insomniac. He would wake up at around two or three
in the morning and then could not get back to sleep. It's strange that
around that time E told me the same thing was happening to him. He
said he would get up at around five, make coffee, and see in the grey
dawn, looking out over the Harlem streets. E would read books in those
hours, about the language of birds, or migration of plants and insects.
J would meditate, or stare at one of his Buddhist philosophy books.

I had no problems with sleeping, though occasionally I would hear
J moving about in his bedroom in the small hours. Sometimes, I would
hear the door of our child's room opening, and hear the padding of feet
into J's bedroom or mine. Or a rare night, the trains would stir me (the
house is right next to the railway). But apart from that my nights were
unconsciousness, punctuated by fragments of dreams.

The fear of never being able to lose consciousness again, eternal
insomnia, is a kind of nightmare. The idea of a god, Morpheus, who
looks over us, and ensures we slip into slumber, attracts me. In sleep
I am released from time. It's often in my sleep that I remember my
childhood days, of walking through the hills, looking for young bamboo shoots, or wading into little creeks to fish out shrimp with a plastic bottle. My world now is so urban. The sounds here are not those

of my childhood, like croaking frogs or night cicadas, but rather the mechanical – the drone of cars, or the rumble of a train.

Morpheus is a shape-shifter, changing the stability of our mundane reality. One of the most mysterious of Goya's etchings is entitled *The Sleep of Reason Produces Monsters*. Is the god of sleep looking at what he can do to the poor man, in the form of bats and owls? Or is the god in the head of the sleeping man, and his dreams accompanied by those nocturnal creatures?

Goya's etching is immensely powerful, though I am not sure why exactly. There is something about the man's tights and tiny, elegant shoes. His tangled mop of hair. The cat looks like a feline out of Lewis Carroll. The man is besieged but sunk in sleep, having lost the power of bodily agency. The etched glow suggests twilight, a kind of dream light. Both J and I like this image so much that we have made a copy that hangs in our living room, above the TV, which is a fitting place for it.

Walking Backwards / In Reverse
倒走

One of the most characteristic morning exercises in China is walking backwards. If you were in a city park, or on a village path, you would be very likely to see people practising this. My father did it almost every morning, along with his qigong exercises. He would walk backwards in a flat field, slow but steady. Before he died of cancer, he came to visit me in London. And he did it here in the mornings – walking backwards in a quiet street near Bethnal Green. But I barely see anyone doing this in the West.

Walking forwards is an automatic movement, but walking backwards is a conscious effort, an activity that requires forgotten muscles to coordinate in order to cope with this mind–body challenge.

Endorphins
内啡肽 / 腦內啡

Contracted from 'endogenous morphine'. Derived from Greek ἔνδον / éndon meaning 'within', and morphine, from Morpheus (Μορφεύς Morpheús), the god of dreams in Greek mythology.

I have always liked the word *endorphin*. It's silly, but it makes me think of dolphins, and of the sea. But really it has to do with the body and its response to physical stress or exertion. The Greek root of *endorphin* can be translated as 'inner dream', or 'god of dreams'. Maybe this means the body's inner dream, the sense in which the body has its own internal logic or instincts. I started jogging as a way of dealing with my winter blues, a slight depression due to those grey monotonous months in England. A daily jog allows me to break through the low clouds above my head. I know that if I run till I sweat, I feel energised during the day. After some months I discovered that some days, though not all, after a longish run and a shower, I would feel a buzzing sensation throughout my body. A mild euphoria. It was as if my body was humming an elusive tune, like a gentle drug inside me, buoying me up. Was this the endorphins released into my bloodstream, the inner dream? I realised my body had its own wisdom and benevolence.

Melancholia
忧愁

Melancholia as an illness with particular mental and physical symptoms is described in the fourth century BC. Hippocrates, in his *Aphorisms*, characterises it as 'fears and despondencies, if they last a long time'.

The Anatomy of Melancholy is a book by the seventeenth-century Oxford scholar Robert Burton. In the preface he writes: 'I write of melancholy by being busy to avoid melancholy.'

The word 忧愁 – *you chou* – became a popular concept among young Chinese intellectuals in the 1990s. The expression had almost gone out of use during Mao's revolution, as it was not an 'official' mood and therefore frowned upon. But the word became fashionable again in post-Mao society, partly due to the Chinese translation of Françoise Sagan's *Bonjour Tristesse*. The novel was translated in 1987 by the prominent French scholar and professor Yu Zhongxian and published by a top state publishing house. It had huge sales in the years that followed. In 1990s Beijing, if an artist or writer never expressed the *you chou*, he or she must be a mediocre state artist. Or worse, a newly arrived entrepreneur, someone driven by commerce not creativity.

My favourite image of melancholia in the West is the painting *Isle of the Dead* by Arnold Böcklin. The gate of death is somehow peaceful and even desirable in that depiction. The pale-coloured cliffs, the ghostly looking cypress trees, the boat, the devil and the dead. It's an eternal return, but a return to the timeless. Böcklin painted many versions of this image. And he called these works *Die Gräberinsel* – Tomb Island.

Part of the reason I love this painting is that the tomb island looks like the fishing village where I grew up with my grandparents. The village of Shitang where all the stone houses were built on hilltops, surrounded by the East China Sea. The villagers of Shitang almost always lived their whole life there. Some tried to leave, and a few succeeded. I left. Having left, no one returns to that village, in life at least. The only return would be in death.

Teardrops
泪

Salty liquid from the glands of a person's eyes.

E wrote to me about his eyes. His vision was blurry and his eyes were watery and red. They got worse each day. He carried packs of tissues around all the time, and had to wipe them non-stop. They hurt, he said. The blocked eye ducts got infected. He had to see a doctor.

It started after I left, he said. It was probably hay fever, or some allergy he didn't understand. When I left, it was spring, and pollen filled the air along Riverside Drive. Then he wrote: 'You asked me if I ever cried in my adult life. I can't remember. But in the last few months I could not stop this weeping.'

I remember in my village when I was young, people often pointed to a tree with oily sap on the bark and said they were teardrops of the tree. But if a tree had too many teardrops it would attract many insects and parasites, and the tree would probably never see its next spring. And now, as I was thinking about E's tears, I thought about next spring, and whether we would meet again.

11

Radical: 土

(earth, soil, land)

Nostalgie de la boue / Nostalgia for the Mud / Longing for the Dirt
怀旧 / 寻根

Apparently, the phrase was coined in 1855 by French dramatist Émile Augier.

In the last part of *Lady Chatterley's Lover*, Connie finally confesses to her invalid husband Sir Clifford that she is in love with their game-keeper, an elemental man of the woods. Even though her husband knows this from the beginning, he cannot bear to face the horrible fact that his wife could 'love' a foul beast. He is so furious that he shouts at her: 'You're one of those half-insane, perverted women who must run after depravity, the *nostalgie de la boue.*'

The wealthy Englishman is so enraged that he has to use this French expression in a torrent of abuse. *Nostalgie de la boue* – nostalgia for the mud! Couldn't D. H. Lawrence find anything equally incisive in English? A longing for mud is a longing for one's roots, a supposedly regressive desire to return to one's low origins. The husband refuses to understand the passion of sexual love. Perhaps it is not surprising that a deeply wounded English gentleman would throw such an insult upon the most important possession on his estate.

But I am not sure if Connie, the once elegant and tender Lady Chatterley, is Sir Clifford's most important possession. I suspect the mines he owns are his most prized chattel. Black coal, that's where the passion and money lie. Under the earth. In the darkness. That is where the essence is. All the same – *nostalgie de la boue!*

Soil
泥

Based on Latin sucula, solum – ground.

Every day I looked at my fingers. They were black. Covered in dirt. No, not dirt. Soil, deep under my fingernails. On my palms. I was spending most of my time in my garden. I worked with soil, this mix of organic and inorganic materials, the decayed remains of plants and animals.

I could not bear to be inside. I preferred to be exposed to dirt and dust, even though I knew the chemical layer of soil – the inorganic part – might be mixed in my flowerpots, under my feet, hurting my skin, damaging my health.

I have seen people grow vegetables on landfills, especially in the Chinese countryside. Beans, cabbages and melons. And I have seen it in Europe too. Landfills contain large amounts of toxic heavy metals. Do not grow vegetables on landfill! I want to shout whenever I see this. Grow trees instead! Just as Xenophon, the ancient Greek philosopher said: 'To be a successful farmer one must first know the nature of the soil.' I wondered if I knew my soil well enough.

Witch Hazel
金缕梅

A shrub with fragrant yellow flowers, widely grown as an ornamental plant. American species flower in autumn. Chinese species flower in winter, with red blossoms.

It's also called wych elm, a European type of flowering tree with large rough leaves. Its Latin name is Hamamelis.

A garden is a burial ground, even though its purpose is to grow things. A real garden is full of death and rebirth. A garden without signs of death is not a real garden.

After I returned from America, I wrote to E and asked: What would you like to be in my garden, as a reincarnation?

I hope he didn't mind that I used an improper word 'reincarnation', but that was the word that came into my mind then.

A witch hazel, he responded, because it was a tree he grew up with as a child. It was a tree that stood in his family garden, he explained.

It wasn't easy to find a witch hazel plant for sale. I could not find it in my neighbourhood, not even in a garden centre, not unless I was willing to wait for months. After days of searching, I bought one on the internet. The tiny little shrub arrived, weak and fragile, with only four purple-brown leaves, all wrinkled and curled up. I planted it in a clay pot, and didn't feel very optimistic about it.

Every day I looked at the little witch hazel, especially during the morning and evening. I studied its branches and cut a little bit more off each tip. The root ball was damaged upon arrival, crushed in the post. It might die soon, I thought to myself, but without telling E. I watered it every day and gave it a layer of compost. The soil was always wet (too much water and love, I reflected later). One morning, after about two weeks, I found it dead. Well, one cannot pronounce the death of a plant at a specific time. A plant does not have a heart. Towering above the black remains, I asked myself, is it totally dead or partially dead? But even if it was only partially dead, why quench my thirsty eyes (and my thirsty heart) every day on such a tiny weak thing? I reached down, pulled the little skeleton from the clay pot, and laid it on the stone ground. It is better to confront its death by terminating it, I thought. By uprooting it. At least that's absolute.

I stopped reporting back to E about the growth of the hazel. 'Reincarnation' means a new 'life' after death, but the death of what? The death of my relationship with E or the plant? E had never seen my garden. And I doubted he ever would.

One evening he sent me a few lines from a poem by Marie de France. It is about Tristan and Isolde: 'The Honeysuckle and the Hazel'.

> *With the two of them it was just*
> *as it was with the honeysuckle*
> *that attaches itself to the hazel tree:*
> *when it has wound and attached*
> *and worked itself around the trunk,*
> *the two can survive together;*
> *but if someone tries to separate them,*
> *the hazel dies quickly*
> *and the honeysuckle with it.*

I thought about the last line of the poem: 'You cannot live without me, nor I without you.' But the truth is, often when a robust honeysuckle attaches itself onto a hazel tree and keeps growing, it eventually kills the host by depriving it of organic life.

Keine Rose ohne Dornen
只要是玫瑰就有荆棘

A German saying: no rose without thorns.

Britain was becoming warmer and warmer. With so much sunlight and so much growth in my backyard, I had to rearrange the plants in order to make a vertical garden. I ended up climbing up and down a ladder. What a contrast with New York, where it had been raining for weeks E told me. It could have been the other way around.

I spent a whole morning tying strings for rose bushes to climb the wall. And a few hours later I found thorns all over my arms. Red scratches covered my skin and they were bleeding. When I came back to the kitchen, and made some tea, I wrote to E. I still carried out this ritual of writing to him every day before noon, when he woke up in America. I told him about my hands and arms, and that I am allergic to rose thorns, a curse for a passionate gardener. Yet I knew he was suffering from the 'weeping hands'. His eczema was torturing him.

I cooked some ready-made dumplings, and after lunch, I saw that he had written back: 'Sorry to hear about your wounds. It's a hazard, comes with your passion. But I'd say: Keine Rose ohne Dornen.'

Dialect

方言

From French dialecte, via Latin from Greek dialektos, 'discourse, way of speaking'.

In Chinese, dialect is 方言 – fang yan – local speech.

At the conclusion of a lecture given by the sociolinguist and Yiddish scholar Max Weinreich in New York in the 1940s, someone in the audience asked him about the difference between a language and a dialect. Before the scholar could even answer, one of the audience members proposed that a language is a dialect with an army and a navy.

This is a great answer. When a dialect becomes an official language, that's when power and a certain social structure are affirmed. In modern China, the national language is based on the local speech around the region of Hebei, in the northern part of the country. And Beijing is the centre of that area.

In the village in South East China where I grew up, Haikka was the local speech. My grandparents and I spoke to each other in that language. When my grandparents died, the Haikka language died in me. I left the village for a town where everyone spoke Wenling dialect. The two dialects are totally different and I had to learn the new one. It was a long time before I could speak Mandarin, the official language.

Haikka literally means guest people. I never really learned where my ancestors came from. In the 1980s, my father travelled to a village called Baiqi in Fujian Province, where his father's family had lived. In that community there were only women and children. The men had died or left for the cities. Most of the women were widows, wearing black. My father found the graveyards of his ancestors. Almost everyone in that village was related to the Guo family.

Years have passed, and I still have not been to this ancestral place – a supposed 'original home', a windy village near the Taiwan Strait. What's more, I have completely forgotten my Haikka dialect. Do I feel ashamed of having lost my first language? I feel neither shame nor regret, but a sense of nostalgia. Perhaps Haikka is typical of a language that gained no power, because it had neither an army nor a navy behind it. All that remains are memories from individuals scattered in literature, and in oral history. Occasionally I encounter the dialect (now a distantly familiar sound) in a Chinese restaurant in Paris, or in an Asian community in San Francisco.

The Yellow Peril / Die Gelbe Gefahr / Le Péril Jaune
黄祸

A racist view towards East Asian people, representing the Western fear of Chinese culture.

The term 'yellow peril' was not an English expression originally. It might have come from French or German. Some believe the Russian sociologist Jacques Novikow coined the term in 1897 in his essay 'Le Péril Jaune'. His idea was taken up by German emperor, Kaiser Wilhelm II. The German orientalist and diplomat Max von Brandt also suggested that imperial Germany had colonial interests to pursue in the Far East, and the Kaiser adopted the term *die gelbe Gefahr* to encourage the European empires to invade and colonise China. The last German emperor was infamous for his xenophobic views of the Chinese.

We know, however, that the idea of a yellow peril (or yellow terror) goes back much earlier. It can be traced as far back as the Mongol Empire's invasion of the West in the thirteenth century. Then the Opium Wars in the nineteenth century between the English and the Chinese reinforced the hostile image. But the concept became an established part of Western ideology only around the 1920s. It was when American eugenicist Lothrop Stoddard published his book *The Rising Tide of Color Against White World-Supremacy*. Stoddard was a white supremacist and nationalist who wrote several books advocating eugenics and scientific racism. He was also a member of the American Eugenics Society and, not surprisingly, the Ku Klux Klan. Stoddard's book was a success. Even the *New York Times* praised the work when it was released. In 1921, President Warren Harding referenced it to support his segregationist views in a speech in Alabama: 'Whoever will take the time to read and ponder Mr. Lothrop Stoddard's book on *The Rising Tide of Color . . .* must realize that our race problem here in the United States is only a phase of a race issue that the whole world confronts.'

Stoddard's works influenced the Nazi government in Germany. His other book, *The Revolt Against Civilization: The Menace of the Underman* (1922), introduced the term *Untermensch* into Nazi ideology. This clearly chimed with the Nazis' interpretation of Nietzsche's idea of the *Übermensch* or overman. For Stoddard, 'yellow races' and black people are under-men (*Untermenschen*), and so are the Jews. Hitler had come to similar conclusions during Stoddard's time.

This Western ideology entered into mainstream culture on a big scale. English novelist Sax Rohmer published the first Fu Manchu novel in 1912. He sold 20 million copies in his lifetime. The popular 1930s comic strip *Flash Gordon* portrays the planet Mongo as ruled by an evil emperor named Ming. The white people are the heroes coming to earth to rescue the innocent. Despite such a racist depiction, in 1996 the series was selected for preservation in the US National Film Registry by the Library of Congress as being 'culturally, historically, or aesthetically significant'. So was *Birth of a Nation* by D.W. Griffith, a seriously white-supremacist work. I remember watching *Birth of a Nation* at film school in China, and falling asleep after a few minutes just like the rest of my classmates. At that time I was not sensitive to its political implications, and I had never heard of the Fu Manchu series until I came to Britain.

Withdraw

撤回

Middle English: from the prefix with, 'away', + the verb draw.

Like watching a play, scenes from New York ran through my mind as I walked the London streets. In the short time E and I were together, we weren't able to get to all the things we wanted to talk about. We were always in a hurry. We tried to make love before leaving home for the theatre, or to embrace each other in a long kiss in front of the subway. Time and space kept harassing us and telling us to be apart. Heaven was jealous of us, as were unloved ones in the street. Even when we were about to fall asleep at midnight, we still tried to assure each other that our bodies were awake for each other. Words disappeared when our skins touched. Stories were unimportant when we were together. Sometimes, when I lay my head on the pillow I felt exhausted. So did he. I felt the process of my ageing through my often stiff limbs, and I wondered if he felt the same. Though he would not like to admit it. But sex would defy his age, and my age. From the first night when we removed our clothes, I knew his body was receding from his mind. I looked at his naked body, and I thought I would soon leave him. A receding body. *Receding* – wrong word, perhaps? Withdrawing, that's the word he used later. He used the word to describe his sexuality, after we lived together for two weeks. He explained to me that his body was *withdrawing*. But withdrawing from what or who? I asked stupidly. From love, from the woman in front of me, he responded. He talked about being frightened by my love (or by my position when we were making love?). The way I gazed down at him. I realise that the opposite words for *withdraw* are: enter, insert, move forward.

The Pastoral Symphony
贝多芬第六交响乐

Beethoven's Sixth Symphony, completed in 1808.

For a period in my life, before I met J or E, and before I had a child, every summer I would visit south-west Germany. I would spend some time in a village in Baden-Württemberg in the Black Forest. I stayed with a German family in a house surrounded by fields of rye and forests. I worked on my books. In the afternoons, I rambled along the rye fields towards a dark wood in the distance. The silent forest haunted me. I would stand by the edge of the forest, admiring the tall, erect, intense pine trees. It was as if Beethoven's Sixth Symphony was playing in my ears, I felt the pastoral joy of the countryside. I entered deeper into the woods, where the sun could not penetrate through the branches, and even at high noon the forest is dark.

On one afternoon, the sounds and colours changed around me, the rustle of the wind was different. It was as though Beethoven had composed a new movement. Unexpected thunder and lightning menaced the forest from above. Where would I go from here? Return home? For some reason, despite my fear, I stumbled further into the forest. A violent wind shook the treetops above me, as though it would tear out the branches. I saw strange, animal-like shapes leaping about in the canopy above. Gripped by anxiety, I checked my phone to remind myself of time and direction, and cursed my own stupidity. I was desperate to find a path out. I felt the raindrops. I huddled against the base of a great tree trunk for a few minutes, and the storm passed over. The trees calmed, and I managed to find my way out. Under the open sky, the forest gave way to towns and villages, to roads and motorways. And there was neither Schwarzwald nor fear. It was just the final movement of the 'Pastoral' – 'Shepherd's song. Cheerful and thankful feelings after the storm.'

Years later, when I met E, a Beethoven lover, I thought of that forest and the emotion I had felt that afternoon. I told him this story, and explained that I only began to understand Beethoven there, during that storm. It was probably the first time I understood a certain Germanic sensibility through nature and music. I don't know how E would feel if he walked into that wood beside me. Perhaps he would feel at home, and would love that haunted feeling. After listening to my story, E responded: I never had to get caught in a storm to understand Beethoven. But when I think of the Sixth, I always imagine Beethoven deaf under the lightning and thunder.

Clearing
清理

An open space in a forest cleared for cultivation.

My black forest in Germany is a patchwork of dense canopy and areas of 'clearing'. The clearance of parts of the forest allows the locals to gain light and space, so that cultivation becomes possible. At the same time, clearing creates a certain peace and security of mind. I think of a little lake in that black forest. To get to the lake you follow a narrow path, almost impenetrable, tangled brush impeding the way. Then, out of the gloom, the lake appears. Dark water, static, reflecting the trees. Once, I surrendered myself to the water. I felt as if a million eyes watched me from the lake's shores. Not because I was naked; it was more that the surrounding forest suggested a certain secrecy and unknowability. But the open lake gave me a sense of trust and safety. The forest seemed to call to me, or murmur a kind of secret. I think of a lost child in the wood, maybe quietly crying.

The forest lake, hemmed in on all sides, is like a metaphor of life. We are born from darkness; for a period we are bathed in the light; then we move towards the darkness again.

I thought of the Ramble in Central Park. The Ramble is the inverse of my black forest lake. The Ramble is a miniature forest in a vast clearing. The clearing is the city of New York. In the Ramble, I don't feel hemmed in by the city and its millions of eyes. Rather, I feel disembodied peace.

Chimonanthus
蜡梅

Lamei (蜡梅) in Chinese means December blossom, or winter plum. The name *Chimonanthus* is from Greek: kheimōn 'winter' + anthos 'flower'.

Chimonanthus, or lamei, is endemic to China. Though I am sure if one looked hard one could find a flowering *Chimonanthus* beyond Chinese borders. I could imagine a crazed plant lover on a mission to find the legendary scented winter flowers and he or she might eventually encounter it by the riverbank of Amnok in Korea, or next to a lonely cliff in Fujinawa in Japan. One day, I hope, someone will write to me, reporting what I have predicted. I will raise my glass and drink to that news.

Lamei is one of the few flowering trees in China grown solely as an ornamental plant. A unique tree, it demands an exact feng shui when you plant it. A feng shui master or a good gardener will tell you that a position should be chosen where its fragrance can be appreciated while coming and going from the house. The directions of the wind around the house should be considered as well.

The flowers also need some political and social support to survive. After the Great Famine and mass death in the 1950s, Mao and the Communist Party decided that all arable land had to be used to grow crops for the food supply, not for useless flowers. So the gardeners got rid of flowers in the park and grew only vegetables. But somehow lamei trees were never eradicated. Perhaps even Chairman Mao loved the lamei flower – its strong scent, its exquisite beauty. He actually wrote many poems about this winter plant. One famous poem is entitled 'Ode to the Lamei Blossom'. It begins:

Rain and wind accompany winter's departure,
Snow welcomes spring's return.
Even though the cliff's face wears a veil of ice
A flower blossoms pretty and fair.

So the lamei trees continue to thrive. After all, there is something beyond ideological limitation! Nature can indeed win over politics.

III

Lexicon of Enduring

12

Radical: 音

(music, sound, melody)

Leitmotiv / Leitmotif

主旋律

From German: leit – 'leading', motiv – 'motive'.

I was contemplating a young fig tree in my garden, thinking about something I had just read about Wagner. What a turbulent life. Germany before the wars. Exiles and scandals. Wedlock and betrayals. Not every artist had such a dramatic and disturbing life. I felt cold, and found myself shivering on the bench. I looked up, clouds had gathered, gusts of wind arrived. I imagined the sky above me was similar to the sky above Wagner's life. Stormy, unstable and ever-changing. I put on my blue raincoat and remained in the garden for a while.

My eyes fell on the fig tree again. Growing in a small clay pot, the fig tree had a strange shape with its forking branches stretching in opposite directions. The structure had a defect that would prevent it growing into a big tree. I regretted that I hadn't trimmed its branches when I bought it two years before. It was a tiny young thing but it was already forked. If I were a professional gardener, I would have cut off the branches just to keep the trunk growing. As it was, it developed only horizontally in my vertical garden. As I studied the fig, I noticed a plant growing in between the two fig branches that I hadn't seen before. Its root was an avocado stone split in two, and that was where a small avocado sprout shot up.

It took me a while to realise where the avocado stone came from – it was from the plane I took from JFK to London. It was originally from E's kitchen in his New York apartment. Now it had begun to reproduce itself, but on the roots of my fig tree.

I stared at the hybrid fig–avocado plant, and wondered about the composer again. Wagner's last wife, Cosima, was the product of elite European intelligentsia. Her mother was the woman who inspired Dumas to write *The Lady of Camellias*: Countess Marie d'Agoult. After her affair with Dumas, she then lived with Franz Liszt and gave birth to Cosima, who later married Wagner.

It seems to be a formula that women provide men with inspiration, and then men write about their romance. Though in Wagner's case, women are more symbolic than real. In his operas, there is not much domestic or social reality about the women characters, but plenty of angst born of desire and morality.

Then I thought of the night when E and I saw *La Traviata*. The exquisite white camellia curtain, the adored stage, the fragile dying fallen woman, my tears in the dark, and our hands holding together.

The wind was gone. Dusk arrived. It reminded me that I was at home in London. My eyes returned to the fig–avocado plant. The garden was cast in a soft blue shadowy light. A sweet and slightly burnt smell was coming out from the kitchen. I realised that J was frying plantains again.

Liebestod – love death
情死

'Liebestod' is the title of the final aria of *Tristan und Isolde* by Richard Wagner.

During her six-year romantic connection with Wagner, the poetess Mathilde Wesendonck lived on the ground floor of her villa in Zurich, facing the garden. Wagner lived upstairs. Then, Wagner was still married to his first wife, and Liszt's daughter Cosima had not entered the scene yet. The villa belonged to Mathilde and her husband Otto Wesendonck, a silk merchant. In those days, merchants were never home. How would a lady fill her time on a large estate while her husband was on a horse cart with his servants in China or Burma purchasing silk? Obviously she took in the men who amused her. And Wagner grew more and more attached to the poetess.

The love that flourished in that villa inspired Wagner to put aside his work on *Der Ring des Nibelungen*, which would not be resumed for the next twelve years. He began to work on *Tristan und Isolde*, which was based on an old European myth. The original version portrays the tragic adulterous love between the Cornish knight Tristan and the Irish princess Iseult. But Wagner reinvented his version, with a much more philosophical dimension. How exactly did he translate the philosophy of Arthur Schopenhauer into his musical composition? What was going through his mind? Was it for him always meaning first, melody second? Or was there no such separation in the thoughts of an experimental composer like him in his time? After all, he was not Liszt, whose fame came from his fingers. Wagner wrote epic operas. Which for him meant a new music, a new narrative, and a new form that would bridge philosophy, music and storytelling. It was full-blooded music, with passion and a tragic outlook. It would prevail over other musical forms, Wagner believed.

How much does art mirror life, or vice versa? The two lovers simply could not survive their stormy love; they had to die. *Liebestod* – love-death – the leitmotif of Wagner. Perhaps the myth of Tristan and Isolde is about their inseparable nature. When they die, they are buried in different graves. But from Tristan's grave grows a scrambling briar, and from Isolde's grows a rose tree. The two plants intertwine. Just as in the poem by Marie de France that E sent to me, a *lai*.

In real life, Wagner did not die of love for a woman. Though he had to leave the poetess and her villa. His wife was aggressively pursuing him. He first hid himself in Venice, and then returned to Switzerland but not to the villa while finishing the third act of the opera. He wrote the death of *Tristan und Isolde* totally alone, without his wife or his muse beside him. Perhaps only a man whose love has been annihilated could write such a tragic ending.

Traumsprache
梦语

Traumsprache is the word Sigmund Freud uses in his writings on psychoanalysis.

When I say dream language, I don't mean the verbal language or speech in dreams. I mean the images and scenes that drive it. We dream in the non-verbal language of the unconscious. It is only when we wake up, and try to recount the dream, that we adopt a verbal language to articulate it.

Freud, in his *Introduction to Psychoanalysis*, saw a similarity between the image-and-thought-based Chinese language and dream language. He believed that the Chinese language is an excellent medium for the expression of thought. He was especially fascinated by the quality of vagueness in this ancient language: its utter simplicity of grammar, its non-explicitness, its context dependence. The Chinese language is one of the oldest languages yet is still spoken by such a large population today. Therefore, Freud thought there must be a deep underlying structure to enable such a long tradition. He also noted that the Chinese language has no grammar and is based on ideograms and images, suggesting a closeness to the structure of the unconscious. In his own words: 'In spite of this indefiniteness, we have been assured that the Chinese language is a quite excellent vehicle for the expression of thought.'

Jacques Lacan studied Chinese with the Chinese-French writer François Cheng in the sixties in Paris. He explored this supposed connection between the oriental language and the unconscious. And he found the inner connection between the two, which led him to state humorously that if he was a Lacanian it was because he once studied Chinese.

I wonder if Freud was interested in the ancient Chinese philosopher Zhaungzi, who wrote about himself being a butterfly in a dream. In one of his philosophical pieces, 齊物論: 'Discourse on All Things Equal', Zhuangzi wrote:

> *Dreamers of wine drinking often sigh with the coming of the dawn; but the one whose dreams are filled with sighing may set off to hunt at first light.*
>
> *The dreamer does not know he is dreaming, but he may still dream of a dream and what it means.*
>
> *And upon waking he may still not know it was a dream. But the day will come when we shall all wake and know we have awoken from a great dream.*

But Zhuangzi was a Taoist, and he was not preoccupied with analysing a man's unconscious. A mystic who lived in the woods, Zhuangzi was more interested in how a man and a butterfly can be morphed into one being, one cosmic flow, rather than dividing them.

Liebesträume

爱梦

German for 'love dreams'; it is also the name of a piano work
by Franz Liszt.

The German word *Liebesträume* is so beguiling, I thought.

I had been listening to the three piano pieces by Liszt.

Only recently I learned that the three pieces were based on three
poems. It was a surprise to me. Liszt's piano compositions are never
simple or minimal, they sound elaborate and tortuous to my untrained
ears. And I always thought great music could escape from literary texts.
But that's not true. Not even Liszt.

The poems depict three different forms of love. They are *Hohe Liebe* –
exalted love, *Seliger Tod* – blessed death, and *O Lieb, solang du lieben
kannst!* – love as long as you can! When music is composed for a narrative text, it demands a different way of listening to it. What interests me
most is the second piece – the ethereal piano trying to convey the idea
of the blessed death, or erotic love. The opening line of Uhland's poem
is '*Gestorben war ich*', 'I had died'. It seems to be a common thought that
erotic love is 'a little death' – *une petite mort*, as the French say.

I try to think of an equivalent expression in Chinese. This well-
known verse from a Yuan Dynasty poem comes to mind. It expresses
a man's sexual desire and passion:

牡丹花下死，做鬼也风流
*Best to die under the peony flower and become a ghost of the
scented wind.*

One of the most popular traditional operas in China is *The Peony Pavilion*. Written four hundred years ago, it is perhaps the most romantic and tragic story in Chinese literature. But if Liszt had known this story, perhaps his interpretation of *Liebesträume* might have been different, or would even be reinforced in his composition.

The story is a Chinese love dream, or multiple dreams. Sixteen-year-old Lady Du walks into her garden and falls asleep under a tree. In her dream, she meets a young scholar. She falls deeply in love with him. A petal falls onto her hair and wakes her up. She then enters a sorrowful trance and all she can do is to return to the dream so that she can be unified with her lover. The two lovers have never met in reality. But in her dreams they overcome all difficulties, transcending time and space, life and death, and finally find themselves together. Lady Du's revival is always in the garden, by the peony pavilion.

The opera has a total of fifty-five scenes, and sometimes runs for twenty-two hours onstage. When I was a child, there was an outdoor makeshift stage by the village market where the opera was performed every year. The locals would sit by the stage to watch the scenes in sequence every afternoon, while eating red-bean cakes, or sunflower seeds. Plenty of green tea would be served. Perhaps some of the women watching entered their own *Liebestraum* in those moments at the market, but I was too young to understand the love dream and why it was so sorrowful. I never experienced those scenes again after I left my village for the city. And in later days I began to compose my own love dreams, my own kind of *Liebesträume*, often in a written form.

Mauvais Sang
怀血

French, bad blood. It's a chapter title from Rimbaud's poem *Une Saison en enfer* (*A Season in Hell*).

When I hear Liszt's piano pieces on love, and the Chinese opera *The Peony Pavilion*, I think of Rimbaud's life and his poems. Almost every paragraph in 'Mauvais sang' suggests the intensity of burning youth, a desperate need for clarification of faith and love. In this section from *A Season in Hell*, the lines are painfully dancing, feverish and occasionally sober:

> *I shall return with limbs of iron, dark skin and wild eyes. By my mask, I shall be thought one of a mighty race. I shall have gold. I shall be leisured and brutal. Women love to look after these ferocious invalids, back from the tropics. I will become involved in politics. Saved. Now I am accursed, I detest my native land. The best thing is a drunken sleep, stretched out on some strip of shore.*

What does Rimbaud mean by 'I shall be thought one of a mighty race'? Did he mean he would be reborn with strength after returning to France from Africa? Did he really believe politics or revolution would save an enraged soul? He probably did – any poetic and radical teenager would. Then:

> *Do I understand nature? Do I understand myself? No more words. I shroud dead men in my stomach . . . Shouts, drums, dance, dance, dance!*

It is hard to imagine a poet could produce such lines without drugs or excessive alcohol, even a genius like Rimbaud. The mind and the body can be consumed and ultimately destroyed by the distilled liquid, until one day the creative mind gives up. And in Rimbaud's case, that process was very brief. He stopped writing when he was twenty-one. This verb 'stopped' could be replaced by 'quit', 'gave up', 'abandoned', 'retired', or indeed 'finished'.

Filling Up, Finish, Full

完

完 – wan – is one of the most common 500 Chinese characters in use.

Marguerite Duras said that most of the books that are rejected by editors are overwritten. She stated this a few times in different ways in her various essays. In 'Me and Other Writing', for example, she writes: '*A novel, written in its fullest, should be avoided.*'

I spend some time thinking about what she said, and I agree with her. I think about those overly written, perfectly told yet dead books: countless family sagas, turgid historical fantasies. Most of them are so conventionally told that the active breathing is no longer there, nor the pulsing.

The Chinese character for fullness – 完 (wan) – also means to be used up, finished. To be full is to be dead. There are no more possibilities.

完 is a complex Chinese ideogram, since there is no clear pictorial element in this word, apart from the radical at the top ⼍ representing a roof or a house. To be complete is to fill up the house. How interesting this concept is, especially for a writer. Does the writing process resemble filling a house with things? What if a certain kind of writing is a journey into the world in itself? For me, the creativity in the writing process is to keep the doors of the house open so as to be able to move in and out, and to travel back and forth, but not to be locked in a space stuffed with things. To be a good writer for me also means not to use up all one's resources, at least not in one book. As Duras said, a second Proust would be rejected nowadays.

Paradox
悸论

The curious term 'paradox' is made up of para, which is Greek
for 'contrary', and dox, from doxa, meaning 'opinion'.

I sent E a photo of a very unusual mirage. It was a picture of a vivid
cityscape floating on a desert in western China. The city looks so real
with high- and low-rise buildings, and it hovers above the curved yellow sand in the distance. Why did I send this to him? A mirage is
something fantastical but unreal. Perhaps deep in my unconscious, I
know that our love is a mirage – grand but built in the wind. But in
the moment when I sent it, I didn't censor my thoughts. I just wanted
to arouse him, and to provoke him.

E responded, swiftly: 'I love the picture. It is amazing. But it is a
pure paradox – you cannot show an image of a mirage.'

Paradox? What is he talking about? I read his response one more
time. Maybe he is right.

It's like a twisted knot of opinion, a Möbius strip of thought. The
most famous and perhaps the oldest paradox in the West is Zeno's
Paradox. Zeno, a Greek philosopher from Elea, tried to demonstrate
the impossibility of motion. He argued that in a race with the tortoise
Achilles could never overtake. Achilles allows the tortoise a head start
of a hundred metres. Having given the tortoise this head start, Achilles
can never surpass it, since each time he arrives where it was, the tortoise
has already moved on. He can never catch up to the tortoise. Is this a
paradox? My knot of thought was easily untied. Why can't Achilles just
leap over the doddering tortoise in one vault?

Zeno's supposed paradox did not really help me understand what a paradox is. In fact, it just confused me. I tried to think of a better example. Something from the East. Is there not a paradox at the heart of Buddhism about desire and enlightenment? To achieve enlightenment one must rid oneself of desire. But without desire for enlightenment one cannot attain it. Surely that's a better paradox than a tortoise being run over by a Homeric hero?

The paradox in a woman artist's life is perhaps this: to sustain her life with new energy and creativity she needs inspirations and adventures, but these adventures may destroy the safety and structure she has built around her life. You can argue this applies to a male artist as well. But there is more at stake for a woman who is trying to build an independent way of living for herself in this society. There is more at stake for any person from the margins of mainstream society. What I have really been trying to make is a female life not trapped by domestic duty and patriarchal constraints, one that creates its own imaginative and creative power. Some women have done this before my generation, such as Simone de Beauvoir and Susan Sontag. But not without paying a price. And is this price essential? Or is it just a product of patriarchal

capitalism? Sartre did not pay a price for his free love, but Beauvoir did. All her life she suffered from anxiety which was generated by her relationship with Sartre. And Sontag certainly suffered – we often forget that she was an absent mother for her son. Men seek non-paradoxical freedom. But women cannot do the same in this society. Men can have their family and their freedom. But women struggle to enjoy self-realisation without any countervailing force.

Woodpecker
啄木鸟

The woodpecker family includes the wrynecks, piculets, flickers and sapsuckers.

I am thinking of the Ramble in Central Park again, even though it's so far away. That day we walked there, on a pale-sunned afternoon, just days before I left America. E wore his usual goose down and I was in my fleece coat. Among sycamore and hackberry trees, we found ourselves a wooden bench. The hackberry tree had those heart-shaped leaves. Perfectly heart-shaped. I picked one, and twisted it in my fingers. Some people passed in front of us, jogging or walking with their dogs. They were real locals, the lucky ones who lived close to the park.

We noticed the sound of woodpeckers. A distinct, sharp pecking sound. But we didn't see any in the bushes, nor in the branches above us. And something prompted E to think of a poem by Yeats, and he spoke the famous lines:

> When you are old and grey and full of sleep,
> And nodding by the fire, take down this book,
> And slowly read, and dream of the soft look
> Your eyes had once, and of their shadows deep . . .

This was the first poem in Chinese translation I learned by heart when I was at university. But I had never actually read the original. Which was odd. One would think if one could recite a poem from memory, one would at least have read the original. But so many Western works came to me only in translation. In fact, I believe this is the case for many Asian readers (including many passionate ones) and their understanding of Western literature. Without translation, there would be nothing, not even misunderstanding. There would be only the chasm of a cultural gap.

Another wave of chirping came from a woodpecker somewhere, with a different rhythm and tempo from the one we heard before. Were the two birds trying to communicate? Might they be sending mating signals? E was able to shed some light, and comment on the woodpecker's song. He said mating couples may exchange low-pitched calls, and chicks often make noisy calls from inside their nests in the tree.

On that bench, E and I remained quiet for a while, listening to the bird calls.

It was like an afternoon dream, everything vague and soft, apart from the sharp cries of the woodpeckers. While the mild sun was warming our bodies, E found the Yeats poem on his phone and read out the rest of the stanzas. Listening to its original version and remembering the Chinese translation, the whole poem at last came to me naturally.

I finally understood how sorrowful the poem is, and even more so after I returned to Britain. Time passed, our separation continued. Hair turned greyer and our bodies became stiffer.

13

Radical: 辛

(endurance, bitterness, suffering)

Wollstonecraft

玛丽 · 沃斯通克拉夫特

Mary Wollstonecraft (1759–1797), an English feminist writer, philosopher and author of *A Vindication of the Rights of Woman*.

J likes our neighbourhood more than I do. All these years I have lived in London I have wished to go somewhere else – France, Germany, Greece, Italy or America. But J prefers to move about with his feet locally, and to think about his lectures on Nietzsche. Our child seems to be fully at home here. The neighbourhood is her village: her friends, her school, her playground, her park, her pond, her favourite gozleme shop . . . Where she is rooted, J and I are migrants who have lost their roots. We don't yet know about her future.

For sure, Hackney is not Harlem. Everything *feels* much older here, and every building is stained by rain. The main street in my immediate neighbourhood is called Mare Street. In the old days it was known as *Merestreet*. The word *mere* is from the Old English *mǣre* meaning a boundary – referring to the boundary with the parish of Stepney in north London. It might also be the boundary of a large pond which was once fed by Hackney Brook. But there is no such pond now, only the small Clapton Pond, which I pass often, and a tiny one in Haggerston. Clapton Pond has a fountain and water lilies. It's a typical open space in north-east London, with a gang of young boys on bikes on one side facing a few pensioners sitting on the other.

Mary Wollstonecraft, one of the founding feminist philosophers and mother of Mary Shelley, lived in Mare Street two hundred years ago. It was a cattle field then, with farm houses dotted around St

John's Church. I imagine the farmers milking their cows in barns while Mary Wollstonecraft wrote feverishly on women's rights, before fate came to take her. She died ten days after giving birth to Mary. How would she imagine her former home two hundred years later? Even for a great visionary like Wollstonecraft, it would have been impossible to conjure a siren-plagued high street with chain stores such as JD Sports, TK Maxx, Primark, Wetherspoons, McDonald's and so many supermarkets. I often go into the shops (in particular, 320 Mare Street), to fix my mobile phone or buy computer accessories. Could Wollstonecraft have tweeted her latest political insights? Or would social media have diluted her radicalism?

How does a foreigner end up in a given place, after moving between different lands? Because of a love commitment? Or because of our need to reproduce (as people put it nicely: *putting down roots*)? Or because of work, or the availability of cheap housing? I have no conclusion as to why people end up in one place rather than another. That's because I think our chances are blind, decided by some arbitrary force or power during our reproductive years. But from all the arbitrary factors, one begins to build one's own reasons and strength. And perhaps, eventually, one builds some power over the place and the surrounding community. We are like seeds blown by the wind, that land on some rocky outcrop or muddy plain, and there, thanks to the vagaries of sun and rain and soil, we grow into something. We are all hybrids of inner nature and external accidents.

Qiu Jin

秋瑾

Born in 1875, a Chinese revolutionary and feminist poet.

Compared with Mary Wollstonecraft, Qiu Jin was even more radical. So radical that she became a symbol of martyrdom. She wore
a dagger in her Westernised modern clothes, and practised martial
arts. She wrote feminist poems and revolutionary articles. She joined
many underground anti-Qing movements, and wanted to overthrow
the dying Qing Empire. As a result, she was beheaded by the Manchu
government. Qiu Jin was called China's Joan of Arc.

Her name means autumn gem. She was born in 1875. Empress Dow-
ager Cixi was the head of the imperial Qing court then. Qiu Jin was
from a wealthy family, and had a good education, but grew up with all
the feudal traditions a girl would have to endure at that time. She had
her feet bound. But with the support of her family, Qiu Jin also learned
how to ride a horse, use a sword, write poems and drink wine – activities
that usually only men were permitted. When she was twenty-one, she
married a man from a merchant family. Having produced two children,
she was unhappy and unfulfilled. She left her children and her home to
study in Japan. It was unheard of at that time for a woman with bound
feet to leave her family and her country to go abroad to study.

Japan at the end of the nineteenth century was much more modern
than China. It had been reformed with American and Western ideas.
It was in Japan that Qiu Jin became radicalised. To save her diseased
motherland she thought she must join the revolution. She returned
to China and joined the underground movements to overthrow the

government. She was extremely vocal, writing manifestos and calling for women to stand up for their rights. She was already known as a calligrapher and a poet in her late twenties, but she proclaimed that she would toss aside the ink brush to join the military.

The year before she was taken by the imperial force to be jailed, she was the principal of a school in Zhejiang Province, which focused on physical training for military purposes. All this would be funnelled into the revolution. But when her school's co-founder was executed for attempting to assassinate his Manchu superior, she did not run. She continued with her secret mission. And then one summer day, fate came to her. She was taken to prison and tortured. The Manchu government brought her back to her home town, and there she was beheaded in public. It was 1907, and she was thirty-one. Only five years later, the last emperor of China abdicated. One wonders what would have happened to her if she had managed to stay alive for five more years. Would she have become one of the founding members of the Republic of China?

But even if she had survived a little longer, this radical woman would probably have suffered the same fate. A few years after the dissolution of the Qing Dynasty, the first president of China – Yuan Shikai – restored the monarchy, with himself as the emperor. Here we go. The perpetual grasping for absolute power seems to be at the core of our patriarchal history.

Qiu Jin and Mary Wollstonecraft, both fought for women, both wrote political manifestos, both married and produced children, both died young. They did everything a woman or a man could do for their cause. They were as hard as steel, but at the same time as soft as silk. A line from one of Qiu Jin's poems comes to my mind: *It's hard to trade kerchief and dress for a helmet.*

Canterbury

坎特伯雷

A cathedral city in Kent, England.

Some time after I returned from America, I began to travel, but restrictions forced me to turn my attention to the country I was in. One day I decided to visit Canterbury. For some reason, in all the years I had lived in Britain, I had never before felt the need to go there. But strangely, America had made me nostalgic for some remote past, even though it was a past that did not belong to me.

A train took me to Kent, a place where many refugees land by boat via the Channel. But Canterbury seems to be stuck in the past. The size of the town is perfect for walking. The River Stour divides the city and adds to the alluring quality of the space, though the water looked dark and muted. The famous cathedral and its walled garden were charming, but it was rainy. The drizzle went on for hours. I did not have boots or an umbrella with me. After a night in a very draughty hotel room, I returned to London.

Nevertheless, out of curiosity, I began to read Geoffrey Chaucer, the fourteenth-century English author of *The Canterbury Tales*.

Chaucer's family are recorded as wine merchants as well as shoemakers. They also owned many shops and properties in London and Ipswich. How typical, landlords and shopkeepers! Apparently Chaucer travelled wide and far. With his ear for common speech, he produced poetry we can more or less understand today.

Singing he was, or fluting all the day;
He was as fresh as is the month of May.
Short was his gown, with sleeves long and wide.
Well could he sit on horse, and faire ride.
He coulde songes make, and well indite,
Joust, and eke dance, and well pourtray and write.
So hot he loved, that by nightertale night-time
He slept no more than doth the nightingale.
Courteous he was, lowly, and serviceable,
And carv'd before his father at the table.

I am not sure why I am thinking of Chaucer. Is there a connection between my attempt to write my own personal lexicon and the colloquial language Chaucer used in his tale-telling? Why did he write in the vernacular – a highly unusual enterprise in his time? Were his French and Latin not up to scratch? Or was it because the shopkeeper's son had witnessed a poverty of entertainment in working people's lives? If one could not read French or Latin, how would one kill time during those long nights in England, seven hundred years ago? After all, it was during Chaucer's life that England experienced the great Peasant Revolt. The lower classes were fed up with their conditions.

Whatever the reasons, writers like Chaucer, who wrestled with language, seek a new expression, an exit from the dominant language in their time. They need to create a free space where power has not asserted itself.

St Ives

圣艾夫斯

A coast town in Cornwall, England.

I began to venture out, to see other landscapes and ask myself if I could live there. On day trips, I went to Southend, and Leigh-on-Sea, and Hastings. Sometimes with J and our child, sometimes without them. I walked along the sprawling Thames estuary and stared at the muddy sea. And for a longer trip, I took a train along the ragged coast to Cornwall.

I stayed at a friend's house in Saltings, in St Ives. It sits right on the sandy Porthmeor beach. The house used to be a place for storing herring-packing barrels a century ago. Though that aspect of St Ives's history is no longer visible today.

When I think of salting, I think of the salt marsh in my child-hood village, by the East China Sea. It was a vast yellow-brown rocky beach littered with fishing nets all entangled with kelp beds. On the edge of the marsh, villagers would be sorting out the kelp as well as the salt. The salt would be produced on raised areas on the dock, extracted from large heated containers. Eventually, the crystal substance would be piled up on the ground in little white hills. The salt was coarse, hard, and sold cheaply. I remember the countless salty crabs and pickled shrimps we had to chew in my grandparents' house. But here, in Cornwall, I could not see the salted fish or kelp, only the handsome surfers on the distant waves. If I walked along the coast, I could smell the faint odour of salt through the swaying movements of tall cordgrass. That smell has always brought me nostalgia for my home village, a place and a memory so remote that they might as well be a complete fiction. Here, in St Ives, the landscape does not have power over me. But far away, that village by the China Sea where I grew up, with its salty wind and rocky terrain, still haunts me, even when I am here.

Teignmouth

泰格茅斯

A fishing port in the English county Devon.

A few times, on the train from Paddington Station to the west coast of England, I have passed along the Devonshire coastline, with its beautiful sandy beaches, from Teignmouth to Newton Abbey. Teignmouth looked like a charming seaside town, and while I'd never had a reason to stop there before, I finally decided to visit and see what it was that was drawing me there.

I read that Keats lived in Teignmouth for a while, and wrote his epic poem *Endymion* there. The long poem is divided into four books, each approximately 1,000 lines long. But the most well-known lines are the opening:

> *A thing of beauty is a joy for ever:*
> *Its loveliness increases; it will never*
> *Pass into nothingness; but still will keep*
> *A bower quiet for us, and a sleep*
> *Full of sweet dreams, and health, and quiet breathing.*

Given that Keats died so young, at twenty-six, in what feverish state did he write such a saga? What was going on in Keats's life when he wrote those lines? Was he in love or out of love? Did he know that he had not much time left to finish it? When one reads '*a thing of beauty is a joy for ever*' one thinks he must have been in the middle of some mad love, but as the stanza moves on, the poem reads as a memory, a reflective drama with highs and lows, beauty and sorrow, and ultimately death.

I am fond of that word 'bower' in the fourth line. I am fond of that word, a very particular English word, and I cannot find an equivalent in the Chinese language. There is a similar concept in Chinese: 涼亭 – a sheltering hut. But the Chinese bower is a little wooden structure away from other dwellings. It is in the wild, where a man and a woman might meet, or a man might go there alone, in order to reflect in solitude.

I have made a bower here, in England, with J and our child. Though in different circumstances I would also have made a bower for E in America, as a bowerbird would do. Sticks, leaves, coins, rubber, shining objects, anything I could gather on that land. It is said that bowerbirds have the longest life expectancy of any birds. I wonder if that's because of their sophisticated courtship, and the ability to build a home to encourage mating. That's exactly what we humans have achieved.

Still, after walking around the cobbled streets of Teignmouth for several hours, I decided I would take the train back to London. I felt weightless and rootless here, despite its enchanted seascape and the haunting spirit of Keats upon the tides.

The Irish Sea
爱尔兰海

The sea that separates Ireland and Britain. To the north, the
North Channel runs between Scotland and Northern Ireland.
To the south, it links to the Celtic Sea via St George's Channel,
which runs between Ireland and Pembrokeshire in Wales.

I saw J looking at a timetable for ferries going to Dublin. I was curious.
J is half Irish but he never shows any desire to go to Ireland, where his
father's side of the family come from. He had not grown up there.

'What are you doing?' I asked.

'There's a daily ferry from Liverpool to Dublin,' he answered. 'Maybe
we should go one day, so we can float on the Irish Sea.'

I knew he had become obsessed by the Irish Sea lately.

The Irish Sea had been in the news a lot, because of Brexit. For
me, 'the Irish Sea' had always conjured images of turbid waters from
whose depths names such as Yeats and James Joyce surfaced. A non-
European like me does not automatically think of the history of
invasions across the Irish Sea from England.

But since the Referendum, this small body of water had become
the focus of heated debate. The British Parliament, Downing Street,
the EU, everyone on the isle of Ireland and the daily airwaves are
all talking about it. It seems to be a never-ending debate. The phrase
'Irish border' conjures 'chaos' or 'war'. The Irish Sea has become a liquid
mass of contradictions. It has become as complicated as another aquatic
contradiction, the English Channel, which has likewise been churned
up by the Referendum. The Referendum has stripped both of their

romantic and poetic dimensions. The fences around the Channel have always been there, and it looks like they will never be removed unless there is a revolution. Now they want to build fences in the Irish Sea. Surely that's not a symbol of success but of utter failure in statecraft.

J and I didn't go in the end. Perhaps his desire for his old ancestral country was not so strong after all. Perhaps he did not want to tempt fate on the turbulent waters separating his English from his Irish identity.

Minor / Minority

次要 / 少数

From Latin, 'smaller, less'; related to minuere, 'lessen'.

When I was at school in China, I often needed to fill out forms about my family background. For 'ethnic background' there were always two boxes to choose from: *Han* or *Minority*. I would tick 'Minority', as my family was Hui Muslim even though they didn't practise religious rituals. But I had no understanding of what 'minority' meant, since we all wore the same school uniforms and lived in the same building blocks with parents who worked in the same work unit.

Many years later, after I switched my daily speech from Mandarin to English, I began to read literary theory. I read Deleuze and Guattari's essay *Kafka: Toward a Minor Literature*.

As I discovered the truth of my problematic existence, I noted down these lines in my notebook: '*Minor literature does not come from minor language; it is rather that which a minority constructs within a major language.*' I understood that in the case of Kafka, he wrote in High German as a Bohemian living in Prague in what was then Czechoslovakia. He was a minority constructing his literary identity in a major language. I find the essay incredibly relevant; in particular, Deleuze and Guattari ask acute, urgent questions:

> *How many people today live in a language that is not their own?*
> *Or no longer . . . ? This is the problem of immigrants, and espe-*
> *cially of their children, the problem of minorities, the problem of a*
> *minor literature but also a problem for all of us: how to tear a minor*

*literature away from its own language, allowing it to challenge the
language and making it follow a sober revolutionary path? How to
become a nomad and an immigrant and a gypsy in relation to one's
own language?*

The last sentence seems to sum up the reality lived by people like me.
Yes, how to refresh a major language that is so worn out by propaganda
machines? And how to become a nomad and an immigrant in relation
to one's own language? Many people these days have indeed become
nomads in their own languages: Patois English, Creole, or pidgin. Take
pidgin in a Chinese community in San Francisco or in New York, for
example. Pidgin is not the native language of any community, but is
learned as a second language for business communication. Perhaps
an old Chinese chef has no time to reflect upon his learned language
in his windowless basement, but his children might do so. I thought
of writers such as Amos Tutuola who wrote *The Palm-Wine Drinkard*
in pidgin English and the dub poet Linton Kwesi Johnson who wrote
'Inglan is a Bitch' – these works are among my favourite in the English
language. A writer can truly sabotage or reinvent a language which has
been suppressed and ridiculed by colonial sensibility.

Coolie
苦力

A transliteration of the Chinese word 苦力 (pronounced ku-li),
literally 'bitter labourer'.

I remember my first year in England, encountering numerous new
words almost every day. Some were much more surprising than others.
The first time I saw the word 'coolie', I was confused. I thought, huh?
The English have a word that is similar to the Chinese 苦力- bitter
labourer? And it has almost the same pronunciation as the Chinese
term? It took me sometime to realise that the Western word 'coolie' is
indeed a transliteration, or a romanisation of the Chinese word 苦力.

Nevertheless, in English coolie is an offensive word carrying racist
connotations. The word in Chinese has no discriminatory undertone;
it is neutral. It just means labourer, though that's not strong enough.
Perhaps *navvy* is more accurate. In the traditional society of old China,
there were four types of men: hard labourers, farmers, merchants and
mandarin officials. And we know that women belonged to another cat-
egory altogether. So a rickshaw driver in 1930s Shanghai was a coolie.
As was a Chinese railway worker in San Francisco in the 1850s. The
same for a mine extractor from Canto in Peru. Coolies had hard lives,
but obviously not as hard as those of countless Asian slaves in the sugar
plantations of Cuba, Guana Island, Argentina and Peru.

Everywhere you go, you meet the footprints of coolies, even in the
trenches of the world wars in the twentieth century. Just take one place,
say the area around Normandy. There were at least 100,000 coolies
contracted to the British Army during the First World War. They were

sent from east China to the ashes and mud of Europe. They dug mass graves and trenches in northern France and Belgium. They were themselves frequently buried by German bombs. But where are their stories in our history books?

Times have changed and now the Chinese are seen as wealthy people. There is a new Cold War between East and West, the economic war. The Chinese have again become the enemy. So don't expect that the coolies will now get historical justice. Their history will remain buried as a price of Chinese power.

What have the children of former coolies been thinking all these years? In the West, a Chinese face among the black and white crowds is inscrutable. But inscrutability is just a projection of the Western idea of an essential nature of the Chinese, who find themselves frequently bamboozled by the West's social world. We are caught in between the identity of black people and the guilt-ridden talk of well-meaning whites. Often we are caught in the crossfire between these two groups, and our loss of life goes without being mourned or commemorated. Our injuries go without acknowledgement. What we are getting is a rerun of the yellow peril myth. President Xi Jingping is the new Fu Manchu, and Chinese people are seen as industrious but suspicious infiltrates of Western societies. We suffer a new wave of demonisation.

Grow Your Hair and Keep Your Faith (Chinese idiom)

续发明志

> Similar ideas exist in other cultures. Samson, an Israelite warrior, was renowned for the prodigious strength that he derived from his uncut hair.

The growth of my hair is proof that time passes. It's proof of my endurance. So I let my hair grow, trying not to shape it. This is my decision: I will not cut my hair until I see E again. This will be in a year. Or two, or more. Just like a Spartan in ancient Greece, or a martial artist in old China, keeping hair and beard to keep their faith until he fulfils a grand mission, in most cases, a final mission.

Endurance
忍受

From the Latin indurare, 'harden', from in- 'in' + durus 'hard'.

It is killing me, and *it* makes me sigh endlessly. What is *it*? I mean my life here without E, or the deprivation of our physical intimacy. This morning as I was waking up, I became so aroused by the thought of him kissing me from behind, so overwhelmed with wanting him, that I came. When I opened my eyes the morning sun had moved away from the window.

Now being physically together is prevented by an external force. And this state goes on for an unseeable future. Endurance, this is the only word I can think of, for this immovable and numbed hardship.

I miss his body and his lips, and I miss fucking him. I think of one of my most intense memories: sitting on that rattan chair against the window and the incredible force and closeness we had between us.

Good Herbs Taste Bitter (Chinese idiom)
良药苦口

The Chinese idiom 'good herbs taste bitter' refers to the traditional practice of herbal medicine.

Almost every herbal medicine has a bitter flavour due to its being dried and concentrated. Silvery wormwood leaf (*ai ye*) has a bitter, sweet taste. Its warm, yang nature is believed to be good for blood and is therefore beneficial for the liver and the kidneys. White mustard seeds (*bai jie zi*) reduce phlegm and coughing. Powdered woad root (*bai lan gen*) is perhaps the most common herbal medicine you can get in a Chinese store. It's for cooling the blood and preventing inner heat. Goji berries are high in vitamins and minerals and they are good for the immune system. Areca nut (*bin lang*) is the fruit that can expel parasites, and children in the Chinese countryside take it in different forms. Turmeric (*jiang huang*) is good for preventing cancer and invigorating blood circulation. Dried yellow coltsfoot flowers can relieve coughs and wheezes and are therefore good for lungs, and so on. Most dried roots and herbs have a pungent smell. None of them has the specific effects of Western medications. They are more holistic. They are used on a daily basis, more to treat symptoms rather than to cure illnesses. All herbal medicines are just like good vegetables and fruits which nature offers us, as part of its bounty. And we should not waste or ignore this abundance. If we don't know anything about roots and herbs and their curative powers, then we don't understand the relationship between our body and the nature around us.

But for me, life is a disease without a cure; it's a terminal condition. Yes, we can celebrate sustaining our good health. We like the idea of maintaining it for as long as possible. But we all have to drink the bitter herbs of our mortality in the end. In my mind, I can hear J agreeing with me and then quoting from his beloved Nietzsche. Often, he says to me: Now and then, quoting the words of dead philosophers can help you cope with reality, if your medicines do not work.

Then there is love, the sickness in life that we desire and pursue. Lovesickness cannot be cured by medicines, but time might cure it eventually. Although we don't like to admit it, love fades. But what remains afterwards? I ask myself.

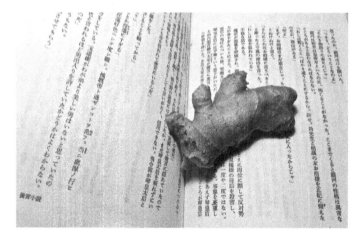

14

Radical: 生

(live, vigour, raw)

Carnivorous
肉食

An animal that feeds on other animals.

Once E said I was 'a carnivorous plant'. I never asked him to elaborate. But I had an idea of what he meant.

Recently I was at a friend's house, and saw a potted Venus flytrap there. I studied the opening of the flower – more a static animal to me than a plant. Yes, a Venus flytrap. The two elongated petals have to close within twenty seconds so that it can trap insects. A flower capable of rapid movement. This seems to be against the supposed immobility of plants. It is movement within an immobile state. Apparently, once an insect is trapped inside, the digestion takes about ten days. After that the prey is reduced to a husk of fibrous substance. The trap reopens, and is ready for reuse.

We are accustomed to animals eating plants, but not plants eating animals. Carnivorous or not carnivorous, all living beings survive in their own particular way. I wonder if E is still scared of me, now that we are apart. A woman is a carnivorous plant that captures the male animal. But it is male desire that is the trap. The man carries in him his own Venus flytrap, which devours him. His mind paints the woman with his own grasping impulse. He holds the woman responsible for managing his own desire. And if he's consumed, it's her doing.

Horticulturist
园艺师

From Latin hortus 'garden' + cultura 'growing, cultivation'.

One day I will write a book about being a horticulturist with the title *I Cultivate*. I feel that since leaving America, I have stopped travelling in the way I used to. I try to cultivate the days, the nights and the soil under my feet. I have grown some new plants. I planted two orange trees, one qunka, two camellias, a gooseberry bush, two olive trees and two beds of lettuce, not to mention beans and rhubarb. I can't move much in my garden.

At the end of Voltaire's *Candide*, a profound philosophy is revealed with beautiful simplicity. The three men (Pangloss, Candide and Martin) come to a farm and see an old Turk taking the fresh air at his door under an orange bower. They ask him about a political event in Constantinople, hoping the local man will know. But the Turk answers that he knows nothing of such events. 'I content myself with sending the fruits of my garden over there for selling,' he says. Nevertheless he invites them into the house, and treats them to candied lemons, oranges, pineapples, pistachios and mocha coffee. (Mocha coffee? I would love to know how it tasted then in Turkey during Voltaire's time.)

Impressed by the old man's offerings, Candide asks the Turk if he has a vast and magnificent estate on which he produces such a variety of fruits.

'No,' the old man replies. 'I have only twenty acres. My children and I cultivate them.'

Yes, my children and I cultivate them. We must not forget to cultivate our garden. And that is all we can do, when nothing else can be done.

Guerrilla Gardening
游击园艺

An act of gardening on land or abandoned sites without legal rights. The earliest recorded use of the term was by Liz Christy and her Green Guerrilla group in 1973 in New York. The group transformed a derelict private lot into a garden.

The last time I went to a cinema was at the Metrograph on the Lower East Side of Manhattan with E. We watched Bresson's *The Devil, Probably*. How grey and sad that film is! We followed the suicidal Charles and his friend Michel, witnessing terrifying scenes of social and environmental destruction. As we walked out into the night, the film's images of burning forests and devastated land haunted us. Towards the East River, the area is rough. The characterless housing projects along FDR Drive felt desolate. Is this really part of glitzy Manhattan, or some godforsaken place? The social housing reminded me of the monstrous new mega cities in China. History repeats itself. Cultures copy each other. And we humans are indeed criminals, capable of manufacturing the grotesque on such a scale.

But perhaps the uglier the place, the more revolutionary it might become. The Lower East Side was the area where the first urban guerrilla gardeners started their activism. In the mid-1970s, a man called Adam Purple created a circular garden around Forsyth Street in an abandoned lot. Ten years later, when it was bulldozed by the City of New York, the yin-yang-shaped garden had overtaken other lots and reached a size of 15,000 square feet. What remains of his 'Garden of Eden'? The guerrilla spirit perhaps. It resonates everywhere in the world, especially in capitalist urban spaces in London, in Chicago, in Berlin, where citizens do not have the 'legal' rights to cultivate even abandoned sites.

If I had to choose my night-time profession, between graffiti artist and guerrilla gardener, I would choose the latter. I would be glad to meet my comrades on a dumping ground at night, on a piss-drenched street corner, spreading sunflower seeds and bean sprouts. It is a poetic form of activism, no less effective than marching the streets with anti-capitalism banners.

Bresson made *The Devil, Probably* in the same year that Adam Purple planted his Garden of Eden. Can that be a pure coincidence? Or were they both products of the zeitgeist, the spirit of the time? The only difference is that Bresson announced our doomed future in a symbolic film, while Purple put Voltaire's words into practice: 'All we can do is to tend our garden.'

Bioturbation

生物积沉互动

From Latin bios, 'life', + turbatio, from turbare, 'disturb'. The
disturbance of sedimentary deposits by living organisms,
especially in watery environments.

The presence of crabs on a beach is a sign of a balanced ecosystem. The
disappearance of the little crawling creatures from the sand is a sign of
a distressed ecosystem.

There used to be a huge
population of Shanghai River
crabs in China. They were sold
in large buckets in the market, a
typical summer-night dish. But
the river crabs are not seen so
much in recent years. These crabs,
which are a pale green-grey colour with furry claws, are found
along the Yangtze River and in lakes in the south-east of China. Like
many other types of sea creatures, the river crabs spend most of their
life in fresh water and return to the sea to breed. During their fourth
or fifth year, in late summer, they migrate downstream towards the
East China Sea. They reach sexual maturity in the tide. After mating
and hatching their eggs, they gradually move back upstream into
fresh water, completing the life cycle.

Once again, I thought of my little crab by the Hudson River. I had watched its movement by the bank during one of my sleepless nights. That was one of the early days in New York. I remember well how I tried to grasp words and meanings in that city, as well as my sense of identity.

Ecofeminism

生态女性主义

The term was coined by the French writer Françoise d'Eaubonne in her book *Le Féminisme ou la Mort* (1974).

For better or for worse, Mother Nature is a universal expression. One can think of the positive in this term, but also the negative, especially the stereotypes and prejudice based on feminine qualities. Mother Nature, or Gaia, is being deprived of space and life these days. It's dying.

Since the 1970s, there has been a new wave of ecofeminism. The core theory of ecofeminism asserts that patriarchal values are embedded in a capitalism that dominates women and degrades nature. As long as capitalism exists, women and nature have no power in the world and the split between nature and culture is reinforced. It has been disturbing though uplifting to see so many schoolchildren becoming eco-warriors in the last decade. But aren't humans part of nature, even as we dominate it? And is this domination actually an illusion?

Silent Spring by Rachel Carson is a perfect ecofeminist text. Enraged by the profit-driven farming industry which had laid down vast amounts of poison on the surface of the Earth, she pointed out most of the birds and insects died as a result of pesticide usage. I thought of my own life in China. Once there was a time when everyone used DDT for farming. Once people washed themselves with it, just as we once used to smear lead paint on our faces. Once there was an old man who took a mouthful of DDT to kill himself. Because he had lost hope in his life. That old man was my grandfather. In my faint memory, he was just a strange, gaunt old man who once drank something bad on the second floor of our tiny house. The details of the first few years of my life spent with him remain very vague.

Some years after my grandfather died, I began to ask how humans could create such poisons on a mass scale. How could they flood the world with them with such ignorance and indifference? How could there be such destruction in the world, such cold-hearted polluting? But as more time passed, I began to think differently. I thought, in fact, this is just the complexity of nature itself.

Nature both creates and destroys. She lets the seagull come and peck out the eyes of the lamb, and she allows the eagle to eat the guts of the whale. She deals with mass extinctions. An asteroid wiped out the dinosaurs 67 million years ago. And further back, 600 million years ago, a small change in temperature annihilated 95 per cent of the species on Earth. Mother Nature has a habit of doing this. She seems to destroy her own children from time to time. Right now we are experiencing biodiversity loss on a vast scale and precipitous climate change. Mother Nature is doing it again, but *through us*. Mother Nature is a bitch. She is the eternally fertile mother, but she is also Kali the destroyer, whether she uses asteroids or humans as her instruments.

So what does ecofeminism mean? It's not that nature (female) is under attack from humanity (male). Nature encompasses both creation and destruction, and we can be the agents of that destruction. Still, that's not an invitation to complacency, or even indifference to the crisis. This particular part of the natural world, the human race, which is contingent and dependent on this planet, may be about to disappear, like a sandcastle on the beach. Nature will remain, humans will no longer be important, and new life will come.

Der Kiez / Viertel
住宅区

German, meaning a living quarter, a neighbourhood.

The image of the man in America has, over time, become blurred. The details of E's face almost disappeared, whether I wanted it to happen or not. But one day, all of sudden, I remembered his smell. Nicotine. That certain tobacco mixed with a type of soap.

His smell, even though it was so remote now. It was the memory from when I first kissed him. Where was that? In his apartment, in Harlem. His nicotine smell had reminded me of another person from a long time ago. And that in turn brought me back to a *Kiez* in Hamburg, a clean-aired and elegant northern German town.

The man in Hamburg lived in a nightlife district in the St Pauli quarter, very close to Reeperbahn. *Der Kiez*, that's how the Germans refer to it. That was the first time I'd been in Germany for a long period. The German man rented an apartment for me in the *Kiez*, and we worked on a film together. The film was about a UFO sighting. At that time I was very interested in supernatural elements, though very primitively. In the evening, when I finished the day's work, I would be left alone. I would walk along the stretchy Reeperbahn, heading towards a Chinese restaurant where the Chinese-looking people spoke only German. Very strange, I thought. *Chinesisches Küche.* You could not find any chillis or anything spicy in German-style *chinesisches Küche*. I would eat my mapo tofu with rice, and often add a stir-fried vegetable dish. Then I would walk home. Home then was either at my rented apartment or at the apartment where the man lived. Either way, I had to pass the red-light district. There I was, a young Asian woman on my own and looking confused, passing under the gaze of the tall drunk German men, and trying to decide where I would end up for the night. And I would make a random decision, to go to the German man's house where there were a few elm trees on the road. We would kiss on his balcony, right after he finished his cigarette, or while he was smoking.

The taste of nicotine. Yes, the same taste. They might have been smoking the same type of tobacco.

What's left in my memory, about these men, about my life in the West? I loved these men and I liked being in the West. But I felt alienated by them too. Though I should use the present tense here. I am living in this progressive past, which is the present. Only China is gone, no longer present.

IV

Lexicon of Impermanence

15

Radical: 死

(death, killing, demise)

Taṇhā

贪爱

A Pāli word, from the Sanskrit tŕṣṇā. It is an important concept in Buddhism, referring to 'thirst, desire, longing, greed or craving'.

Autumn has slipped away, as much as I tried to hold on to it by spending most of my days in the garden. I ate there, read there, planted there and deadheaded the azaleas there. I watched leaves turning yellow. Only the bamboos have retained their steady robust greenness. They stand tall in the English light and rain, having adapted well to this northern landscape. They are stoic. Their migration has been much more successful than mine. But winter has arrived, and I cannot deny it. I close the garden door. It is too cold outside.

With the winter light fading, I feel a heaviness grow in my chest. An unbearable feeling of waiting or wanting something to happen, something big, something that can change all. But the changes in my life come so slowly now, like an old train labouring through the soggy grey English fields, fenced by barbed wire.

Taṇhā is the cause of *dukkha* (suffering, pain, dissatisfaction).

It is interesting that the word *taṇhā* (the root is *tarś-* thirst, desire, wish) is ultimately derived from the root *ters*, meaning 'dry' in certain Indo-European languages. Here are just a few words related to the concept of *taṇhā*: in ancient Greek *térsomai* (to dry), in Gothic *þaursus* (dry), in Old High German *durst* (dry), in English *thirst*.

In traditional Chinese medical practice, a folk doctor would say simple things to his patient. 'Your inner energy is too dry, too fiery,' or the opposite: 'Your inner energy is too wet.' If something is dry, or somebody is dry, then they are in a state of thirst. A dry person needs to be lubricated. Just like parched land is not able to produce lush growth. It needs rain, or some form of love.

Still, an old train passing through a rainy landscape does not seem to promise any new landscape, whether it is a dry sunny land or watery swamp. And my *taṇhā* does not recede.

Samsara

生死, 輪迴, 涅槃

The cycle of death and birth in Buddhism.

Samsara is the nirvana. In the religious sense, samsara ends if a person attains nirvana. But what is the nirvana? Is it the final goal of Buddhism? I stare at the Chinese characters of these two words, wondering if the answer might be found in the strokes:

生 死

生死: life and death. Or it can be translated 'life cycle'. Movement is at the core of the cycle, and samsara is the form of the impermanent. When I cultivate my garden, I so much want my plants to live there, to simply be *alive* permanently. I make sure most of my plants are evergreens, such as jasmines, Japanese rubella, viburnum, dogwoods, climbing roses and honeysuckles. But of course, nothing is permanent. Neither I nor the plants.

Turandot

图兰朵

Puccini's unfinished opera, posthumously completed by Franco Alfano in 1926.

One of the most popular Western operas performed in China was Puccini's *Turandot*, perhaps partly due to its oriental content.

In *Turandot*, the Persian prince is madly in love with the Chinese princess Turandot. Suffering from the intensity of his love, he would do anything to marry her, even risk his life. In order to save him, the three Taoists in the opera dissuade the prince by conveying their view that all temporal things are illusion: 'Turandot does not exist, only Tao exists in this world.'

I love this line. It sums up the fragility of youth and beauty. The prince is not in love with Turandot, a woman he hardly knows. But he is in love with the illusion of a woman, and more so, he is in love with himself in relation to youth and beauty.

I spent some time thinking of this line. I thought of it in New York. And now I think of it in London.

Yes, all the same. E does not exist. Our story does not exist. There is only the little crab I saw by the Hudson River that night. The crab did exist. It was in the river, whether I saw it or not, whether I was by the Hudson or not.

Drowned

溺水

Laertes: Alas, then, she is drowned?
Gertrude: Drowned, drowned.
Laertes: Too much of water hast thou, poor Ophelia. And
therefore I forbid my tears.

Hamlet, Shakespeare

Towards the end of *Hamlet*, Queen Gertrude reports that Ophelia had
fallen from a willow tree by a brook and drowned. She speaks in such
detail, as if she were a witness, or perhaps she is.

There is a willow grows aslant a brook,
That shows his hoar leaves in the glassy stream;
There with fantastic garlands did she come
Of crow-flowers, nettles, daisies, and long purples . . .

What are the long purples? It is believed to be a wild purple orchid
with a prominent spadix, common to various countries of Europe. They
become symbols for Ophelia's death. Then, the slow motion of her
death, witnessed by Shakespearean all-seeing eyes:

Her clothes spread wide;
And, mermaid-like, awhile they bore her up:
Which time she chanted snatches of old tunes;
As one incapable of her own distress,
Or like a creature native and indued
Unto that element . . .

But if Queen Gertrude says that Ophelia appeared 'incapable of her own distress', then Ophelia's drowning is her own choice, her play with life and death. Otherwise why these lines: '*like a creature native and indued / Unto that element*'?

The day Virginia Woolf drowned herself, no one found her. It was 28 March 1941. I don't know if it was a grey English spring day, or if the sky had a pale sun in it. It is believed that she filled her pockets with stones and walked into the River Ouse. Her body was found three weeks later. I have never read anything about the state of her body. Perhaps no one wanted to describe how the flesh appeared after being soaked for weeks in water. Very little is known about the day of her death – her husband found her walking stick and her hat by the riverbank. But her body was washed down to south-east Sussex, where it caught on the trunk of a fallen tree. I find it difficult to imagine. Perhaps the beautiful and poetic image of Ophelia's drowning prevents me from imagining the real – the ever-depressed writer desperately seeking her way out of this miserable world. It is said that some children discovered her body.

I have been to the Ouse only once, with a boyfriend. In my memory, the river was winding and clear. It was summer when we took that trip. We wanted to visit Monk's House, Woolf's country home. We must have been haunted by the idea of death, or death by suicide. I was thirty, and had recently left my own country.

We took our bikes on the train from London. I no longer remember at which station we got off. Kemsing? Lewes? I remember the ride from the station on my blue bike. I was worried about the distance, and the English countryside felt unoccupied to my Chinese eyes. We reached a river, and were about to cross it, when my friend stopped his bike on the bridge. I have no recollection of the bridge, but I remember him saying: 'This is where she drowned herself.' I was shocked. I hadn't known in which river Woolf ended up killing herself. Somehow, Virginia Woolf's suicide for me was part of her body of work, part of literary history, and I could not associate the real brook beneath me with a poetic death. But there I was, looking down on the silver water, the broken branches and leaves stuck in a whirlpool, slowing down the moving mass. I could not comprehend death at that moment. It didn't feel real to me. Now, nearly two decades later, I would not say I have begun to know what it is, but I am able to understand it is real.

In One's Element
本土／适宜的

'. . . like a creature native and indued / Unto that element . . .'
Hamlet, Shakespeare

I still have many things to say about Ophelia's death. Or, rather, about the image of her drowning in the green landscape. I spent some time thinking about these lines from *Hamlet*, spoken by Queen Gertrude: 'like a creature native and indued / Unto that element'.

A creature in its element. An Amazonian in his or her forest hut (before deforestation and industrialised farming). A dolphin in the sea (away from plastic islands and polluted water). A butterfly on flower beds (without pesticide spray). A painter in a sunny olive grove (before cutting off his ear).

When I told E I was writing this book in my garden in the sun, he commented: 'You are in your element.'

Perhaps. In a trivial sense.

I didn't tell him that I would rather leave this country and come to live with him for a while (I can only foresee 'a while'). To do so I would have to abandon my people. And I would have to abandon my vertical garden, the solace of my grey urban life: daisies and dahlias, roses and olive trees, several apple and cherry trees, a premature magnolia, mulberry, orange and juzi trees, and an avocado plant transmigrated in the midst of a fig tree, and finally, four pots of happy bamboos which symbolise the sentimentality of my birth country, my motherland, a land I have never loved but always feel within me.

Yayoi Kusama

草間 彌生

Japanese artist (b. 1929) who works primarily in sculpture and installation, known for her brightly coloured polka dots on nude bodies and on large canvases.

I have been visiting Kusama's exhibition lately. And I have been reading about her too. I am fascinated by her troubled early years in Japan.

Young, furious, but haunted, she desperately wanted to leave Japan. She must have felt deep alienation and suppression in a traditional society. Alone, without anyone's help, and without a functional family, she struggled to finance her plane ticket to America. Having sewn dollar bills into her kimono, she finally escaped. After a year in Seattle, she arrived in New York. She was twenty-nine, the same age as I was when I left China for Britain.

She had a fierce look under her long black hair. It flames out from photos where she is surrounded by American hippies of the 1960s art scene. She was obsessed with dots, which morphed into polka dots later in her career. She painted them on everything: bodies, walls, floors and canvases. She was also a serious provocateur. One of her most controversial performances was at MoMA, when she announced to her audience that it was time for everyone to remove their clothes so she could spread paint across their naked flesh. She was an authentic radical. 'Aggressive' was the word that curators and colleagues used to describe her character, especially in her younger years. But was she really 'an aggressive Asian woman' as the Westerners thought of her?

Or was her ferocity a reaction to her deprived social status as an Asian woman artist in America?

    She used the word 'obliteration' many times to describe her child-hood trauma. Her father was a seed seller who owned farms. Once, she said, she was lying in a field of flowers and suddenly her soul disap-peared, her whole being devoured by flower heads. She was 'obliterated by flowers'. What a powerful description, as obscure as it is for us to really understand. There was deep trauma in her childhood, but we don't know exactly what it was. We know that she came from a broken family, and that her mother would send her to spy on her father hav-ing sex with other women. That led to her lifelong fear of sex. She was clinically depressed, especially during her time in New York, where her work was completely ignored by the critics. She tried to kill herself many times, including once by jumping out of her apartment window. And after her failed New York period she returned to Japan, to a men-tal hospital.

    Classifying her work as 'art brut' is simplistic and unfair. For me she represents the history of womankind. A sexually violated, politically annihilated, socially ignored and emotionally deprived feminine life. One of her works is entitled *Self Obliteration*, which seems to sum up a woman's utter despair, in life, in art, in anything real in the human world.

She was no Yoko Ono. And she didn't meet a John Lennon. She did meet avant-gardist Joseph Cornell, but he didn't save her. He was scared of his own mother. Men! Men have all the power but they often lack courage. As I write about her now, she is ninety-one, and still living in the hospital to which she admitted herself decades ago.

Olga Ivinskaya

奥尔加·伊文斯卡娅

A Russian writer and translator, born in 1912 in Tambov and died in 1995 in Moscow, she is the inspiration for the character Lara in Boris Pasternak's *Doctor Zhivago*.

Kusama makes me think of another woman, Olga Ivinskaya from Russia. Both were tormented. But both survived their torment. Their personal lives were open wounds, bleeding with their particular history, and they had to tend to their wounds every day, as long as they lived.

In October 1949, Stalin's KGB arrived at Olga Ivinskaya's house in Moscow. They arrested her on the grounds of being 'an accomplice to the spy'. Obviously, the state knew well that Ivinskaya was the lover of Boris Pasternak. That she was the muse, the real Lara behind *Doctor Zhivago*. The KGB didn't touch Pasternak then, but Olga was sent to the Gulag for the next five years.

In a 1958 letter to a friend in West Germany, Pasternak confessed that Olga was put in jail on his account, as the secret police hoped that by means of a gruelling interrogation they could extract enough evidence from her to put him on trial. Pasternak felt that he really owed her his life.

It is not clear if Pasternak or the KGB knew that when Olga was arrested she was in the early stages of pregnancy. Months passed in the jail, she was put into an isolation cell and underwent repeated interrogation. She had no knowledge of the whereabouts of Pasternak, and lost all sense of the outside world. One night, six months into her pregnancy, the KGB put her in a jeep with shielded windows and drove her somewhere. When her blindfold was removed, she found herself in a basement morgue, surrounded by corpses. She was left there for the whole night. No one told her anything. The next morning, when the police took her to the jeep and drove her back to the jail, she had a miscarriage.

During those years of interrogation in the gulag, Olga Ivinskaya never said a word to denounce Pasternak. While he stayed in Moscow with his wife and children, under the scrutinising eye of the state. He died of lung cancer in 1960. Olga survived him by thirty-five years, though a large part of her life was spent in prisons.

Just before his death, he wrote the last lines of a poem:

The clock-face wearily ascending.
Eternal, endless is the day,
And the embrace is never-ending.

Ophelia

奥菲利亚 (作为约翰米拉的画像)

A painting by John Everett Millais, a nineteenth-century English artist.

I must be obsessed with this painting. The same painting I mentioned before – Ophelia's drowning, by the English painter John Everett Millais. I first saw it at Tate Britain. It haunted me. I then bought a reproduction and hung it on my wall.

Everything seems to be in this painting: the language of flowers, the abandonment of self in nature, and the eroticism it evokes. Some time ago, I saw a copy of a self-portrait of an Englishwoman. At first, I thought it was a portrait of Virginia Woolf. The woman in the painting looks exactly like Woolf, with her prominent nose and elongated face. But the caption explained that it was a self-portrait by Elizabeth Siddal, who acted as Millais' model for Ophelia. I was taken by surprise. Virginia Woolf or the drowning Ophelia? Why and how did I associate the two images so immediately? I learned that Siddal was a model for the Pre-Raphaelite painters, and her husband was Dante Gabriel Rossetti, the founder of the group. Though Siddal died young, suffering from long-term illness and depression, she did not drown herself like Woolf.

Here we are, life mirrors art. Or art mirrors life. Or they are inseparable for some people.

It is said that Millais first painted the landscape, based on the countryside of Surrey by the Hogsmill River. He built himself a hut by the riverbank in order to study the views. Once he finished the landscape he painted the figure. He had Siddal lie fully clothed in a full bath in his studio at Gower Street in London. She was nineteen then, and died only a decade later.

There is a poem, titled 'Without Her', written by Rossetti and published after Siddal's death:

What of her glass without her? The blank grey
There where the pool is blind of the moon's face.
Her dress without her? The tossed empty space
Of cloud-rack whence the moon has passed away.
Her paths without her? Day's appointed sway
Usurped by desolate night. Her pillowed place
Without her? Tears, ah me! For love's good grace,
And cold forgetfulness of night or day.

I looked again at the painting. The drowning Ophelia. The muddy death. The singing mermaid. So many colours. Colours of flowers and weeds, an imagined spring from a wintery time in a painter's life, as well as the life of a muse. But there is one colour which, to me, didn't belong in the painting. Red. A red poppy (or rose?). Is she holding the red flower? Or is it floating upon her gradually sinking body? I went back to the text in *Hamlet*:

> *There with fantastic garlands did she make*
> *Of crow-flowers, nettles, daisies, and long purples . . .*

So, crow-flowers (yellow), nettles (blue), daisies (white, yellow, pink or purple) and long purples. There is no mention of red flowers. Can death be without the colour of blood? Yes, death by drowning, perhaps.

16

Radical: 史

(history, past, saga)

History
史

From Greek Latin historia, meaning 'finding out', 'narrative'.

The Chinese radical for *history* is 史 – *shĭ* . It is also an independent character. The way it is written has not changed in the last 3,000 years. Perhaps because it serves both as a radical as well as a simple concept, the character remained unchanged even after the simplification of the Chinese writing system in the early twentieth century. It is supposed to be a pictorial sign, though no one seems to know exactly what 史 signifies. So mysterious, it leaves us forever pondering its original creation.

When I think of history, I think of the first ape woman Lucy.

Lucy is a female skeleton (of a fossil hominid) discovered in Ethiopia in 1974. She is only 1.2 metres tall, and is about 3.2 million years old. She is the first *Australopithecus afarensis* skeleton ever discovered. The species is also called 'southern ape', a group of extinct primates closely related to us. Lucy's manner of death was analysed by scientists, who concluded that she fell out of a tree, fully conscious. She landed on the ground feet first, sending such an impact up through her body that it created fractures in her ankles, knees, hip and shoulders. Scientists found only half of her bones.

Archaeologists analysed Lucy's body structure. They found that her diet was plant-based. It seems that Lucy had a conical ribcage, found today in apes such as gorillas, which allows room for a large stomach and the longer intestine needed for digesting voluminous plants.

The Chinese sign 史 for history does not change, and it seems it will never change, but our human species has and will continue to do so.

Ninety-nine per cent of species become extinct, as did Lucy's. But even though Lucy lived a short life, her species survived for at least 700,000 years, more than twice as long as our own species, *Homo sapiens*, has been around. What does that teach us? How many more thousands of years will our species survive?

Genji
源氏

Genji is a character in the 1,000-page novel *Tale of Genji*, by Murasaki Shikibu. It details the life of an ancient Japanese emperor, Hikaru Genji, and his romantic encounters.

Women have always written epic history, even thousands of years ago.

Murasaki Shikibu was a young woman who lived in the eleventh century, somewhere near Kyoto, the ancient Japanese capital. When she began to write, she was only in her twenties. She was newly widowed, and didn't know she was writing the supposed first novel in the world. No one else knew that either.

The traditional silk portraits by ancient painters often present Shikibu with long hair wearing a robe, always alone, either in a pavilion or sitting on a rock in a landscape. Every painting depicts a stack of white silk paper in front of the solitary woman.

Who is this mysterious young lady Shikibu? And what propelled her to narrate a court life? My fascination with her is to do with the solitary nature of a writer's world, especially a woman writer's world. She spent more than a decade writing *The Tale of Genji*, along with a diary and a volume of poetry.

At that time, women in Japan were excluded from learning Chinese, the official written language. But raised in her well-read father's household, Shikibu discovered the Chinese classics. In her diary she wrote about how she learned to read and write from observing her brother's study. Even her father claimed that it was a great pity that his daughter was not born a man.

Feminism was not a concept then, but a female point of view surely existed. Yet strangely, her book is written from the emperor's point of view. The young woman author seems to be hiding behind her pages. Here is the tone of Emperor Genji:

> *It happened when I was very young. I was attracted to a woman.*
> *She was of a sort I have mentioned before, not the most beautiful in*
> *the world. In my youthful frivolity, I did not at first think of making*
> *her my wife. She was someone to visit, not someone who deserved*
> *my full attention. Other places interested me more.*

I wondered what Kyoto looked like 1,000 years ago, what kind of house Shikibu had lived in, and what kind of garden she might have tended. Historically, Kyoto was modelled on the ancient Chinese capital Chang'an. I imagine a cityscape with towers, bridges, courtyards and bamboo gardens. And I picture ladies-in-waiting living in the walled imperial courts, just like Shikibu. Though she was probably one of the few who could compose poetry at that time.

When I left America, I gave E a copy of *The Tale of Genji*. I didn't explain why. For quite a long time, and especially when I lived in Beijing, I had felt like Shikibu, obscure and alone, habitually working on one project after another. My own imperial court was first a brutalist

apartment block in Beijing, then a studio room near the Gare de l'Est in Paris, then various flats in England under the influence of Tory austerity. As I am reflecting on this now, I ask myself: What matters in the end? What do I really care about? Not Europe, not America, not China, not any country or any place, but a space for the pursuit of freedom where I can reflect and write. I think of a room of one's own, described so clearly by Virginia Woolf. A table under a lit lamp where I can materialise thoughts as typed words; a sofa where I can lie down to read and think, attain the unattained. It is the act of writing that matters. Writing will sustain a form of love. And that in itself is a constructive way of enduring daily suffering.

Polymath
博学

From Greek polumathēs, 'having learned much'.

Zhang Heng (張衡), a Chinese polymath from 2,000 years ago, is often compared to Aristotle and Euclid in the West. His portrait adorns a Chinese national postage stamp, just like Her Majesty the Queen on stamps issued by the Royal Mail in Britain, except in China we call it People's Mail. We had to study Zhang Heng's scientific contributions along with learning Communist dogma at school when we were young.

In addition to documenting about 2,500 stars in his extensive star catalogue, Zhang Heng posited theories about the moon and its relationship to the sun. He discussed the moon's sphericity, its illumination by reflected sunlight on one side, and the hidden nature of the other side. He recorded the facts of solar and lunar eclipses. It is beyond our imagination that he could have conceived the nature of the moon then. Zhang Heng was also fascinated with earthquakes. He presented to the Han court what many historians consider to be his most impressive invention, the first seismoscope.

He was also a poet and writer. The first stanza of one of his poems, 四愁诗 (Four Sorrows), goes:

> 我所思兮在太山。欲往从之梁父艰，侧身东望涕沾翰.
> *I think of Tai Mountain, where my longed beauty*
> *Resides. But Lord Liang keeps us long apart;*
> *Looking east, I find tears start.*

It's a common belief among scholars that this is not a love poem, but rather a sorrowful reflection of Zhang's need to be recognised by the emperor. Tai Mountain is where he should be really. In his time, even such a highly accomplished scholar had problems being promoted within the imperial court.

Is it typical that even a great polymath had to be blessed by an emperor or a king, men like Zhang Heng or Leonardo da Vinci? Would the polymath have no chance to use and develop his qualities otherwise? It is said that when da Vinci died, Francis I was beside him, that his hands were held by the king and his last words officially recorded.

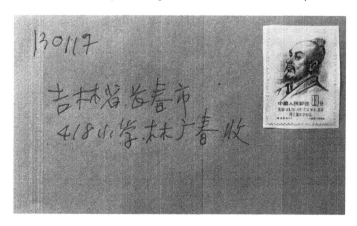

17
Radical: 未

(future, forthcoming, hereafter)

Future

未

From Latin futurus, from the stem fu-, a base meaning 'grow', 'become'.

Since this book is engaged with etymology, I will certainly turn to 未 (*wèi*) – the future – for the final part. Though in Chinese, 未 is a much more vague concept than in English, and contains several different meanings. For example, it can refer to what is uncertain and unknown. In ancient China, *wèi* could mean the early-afternoon hours. (I wonder if that was because the measuring of daytime begins with sunrise, so that afternoon is a forthcoming time. Therefore, the uncertain *wèi*.)

Like the Chinese radical 史 – history – the character 未 has not changed throughout the history of the Chinese writing system. It will remain the same, I guess, as long as Chinese *hanzi* continues to survive. Thousands of years ago, one of the initial meanings for 未 was 'the shape of a tree bush', although that meaning fell away long ago. People found the sign on an oracle bone. The stroke was curved either due to the stone tool used to carve it, or to the shape of the bone. It looks like this: 朱

Individual
个人

From Latin individuus, from in – 'not' + dividuus – 'divisible'.

The Chinese word for individual is a recent construct. It draws on two independent characters, 个 (piece) and 人 (human), in an attempt to find an equivalent for the Western term. Yes, I do think this word is a Western concept. It did not exist in Confucius's China, and it was certainly an insignificant concept during the Communist era. Now, it has been adopted in contemporary China, along with other products imported from the West.

Look at the root of this word: *in-dividual* means *non-divisible*. We have for a long time believed that individuals cannot be divided. A single person is the smallest component of a society, and it cannot be broken down any more. Whereas a village, a tribe, or a family can be divided. But since science and technology have changed us radically in recent decades, the individual seems to be no longer the master of their soul. That power has been taken from us. The workings of our behaviour have

become the business of biotechnology and infotech. Anyone can find themselves in a giant information bank. Our neurons and cells can be coded and categorised by massive processing machines. And our behaviour can be predicted, as if we had been given a well-organised spreadsheet in which to log our choices.

This take on human society sounds cold, and 'inhuman'. Romantics would probably hate such a view. I have always believed that an individual's personality is unique and authentic – it cannot be reduced to codes and numbers in a computer. But am I right? What is *language* doing in our daily life? Can't language be coded and numbered and reorganised, in hundreds and thousands of different forms? And if that's true, isn't my idea of writing a personal lexicon a sentimental project? There could be billions of individual lexicons in this world, and mine is just a bubble on the ocean, a tiny star in the universe.

Big Chill
大寒

A term in the Chinese lunar calendar. Da Han – Big Chill or
Great Cold – is usually around mid-January and it's the day
marking the coldest time of the year. It often refers to the day
when the sun is exactly at the celestial longitude of 300°.

And now it is deep winter. Discontent is soaked in the air, permeating
every corner, like the heavy clouds hanging above Europe. They won't
dissolve for a very long time. Everyone is waiting for the winter solstice
to arrive. For we know once we pass that day, the waking hours will be
longer. And in the slightly longer daylight we will feel better, and better.
I have been waiting for that day. It will mark the end of a very troubled
year. It will replenish my hope of seeing E, or it will terminate my need
to see him in the new year, for better or for worse.

But with the Western calendar, the winter solstice announces the
start of the winter. How hopeless is that? When I think of the Chinese
lunar calendar – *Da Han* is in mid-January – I instantly feel hopeful.
Big Chill marks the end of winter. I then have a completely different
feeling about December and January. Right after the Big Chill comes
the spring. The Chinese New Year is in February; the lunar term *Li
Chun* means Beginning of Spring. Instead of waiting for the spring to
come in April, the East Asians start activities in February.

My separation from E has endured four seasons. I don't know when
we will meet again, or which period of the year it will be. But to think
of the day of the Big Chill, is to think with optimism. From *Da Han* it is
a short walk to spring. I know people have different ways of measuring

degrees of pain, and the length of a separation. But if we think of the seasons, our feelings change. The mind of the season is more powerful than the human mind.

Language is a Virus
语言病毒

In his supposed sci-fi novel *The Ticket That Exploded*, William
S. Burroughs writes 'Language is a virus from outer space'.

Burroughs gives us a dark vision of language. Words have plagued our
minds and now they control us. But we don't recognise this. To quote
Burroughs: '*The word has not been recognized as a virus because it has
achieved a state of stable symbiosis with the host.*'

The language virus has permeated every aspect of our lives. It is
stable yet it mutates. We die, but the virus lives on, spreading far and
wide. I find it strange that for Burroughs the language virus is from
'outer space' rather than an integral element of human life. The very
idea of language infecting us makes no sense if, as Lacan suggested,
we are always and already language. But for Burroughs there was a
paradise in which Adam and Eve lived without language, their minds
in pure and direct contact with each other and the world. Then came
language, in the form of a serpent, and it infected them.

I have a different vision of language. For me, language is everything.
It is my means of escape from the story that was already written before
my arrival in this world. It is my path to freedom. When, as a child,
I first became aware of my surroundings, I found myself living in a
fishing village with my illiterate grandparents. My grandfather did not
speak much, nor did my grandmother. But their physical language – his
violence towards her, her daily prayers before a Buddha's statue – told
me that I should not live in their world nor speak in their tongue. I
left. Later, when I lived with my parents, I discovered my father had

another language – painting. The way he expressed his vision of the world through images revealed to me the possibility of a different kind of language, one that takes the form of art. He showed me that it is possible to choose how to live one's life. After I left my parents, I wrote books and made films. I experimented with new languages. I tried to live the life he showed me was possible. A life based in creation and imagination. To live vividly is to have languages. Not only language in the limited, linguistic sense, but language as an artistic tool, language as art, language as a way to live an authentic life.

Aesthetics

美学

From Greek aisthētikos, 'relating to perceptible things'.

This morning I looked at the wilted hydrangeas in my garden. There were so many dead heads, brown and dried out, bathed in the grey winter light. I took a pair of shears and deadheaded them. While I was chopping them off, I discovered many young buds already growing on the stems. I stopped. Those sprouts were just one or two centimetres below the dead flowers. So intensely green, and so determined to grow, they had attached themselves to the seemingly lifeless stalks. I left the plant, took the dead flower heads and placed them in a vase.

In *The Birth of Tragedy*, Nietzsche argues that the good life has aesthetic value, and the aesthetic justifies our existence. In other words, without art or beauty, life is not worth living. My trivial act of placing the withered hydrangeas in a vase by my bedside is a justification of my daily existence. In the dead of winter, to remind myself of life, these simple moments find some meaning from the blooms of the last year. But also, what I was doing this morning was trying to honour what I had lived through in the previous spring.

Ramble On
漫步

Ramble, related to Middle English ramen, 'to roam', and related to the noun ram. Influenced from Mid-Dutch rammelen, used of animals in the sense 'wander about on heat'.

The Ramble. I think of the winding paths hidden in Central Park. I think of E's winter jacket next to my patterned fleece coat. I think of those tall oaks and elms, as well as the American sycamores by the Ramble. I think of a certain woodpecker making a sharp sound, a bird I have never managed to see.

Mary Shelley's last work before she died was about physical movement. It is titled *Rambles in Germany and Italy*. She wrote about how much she needed to travel, to be away from her depression, to stay away from England. She wrote about her love of travelling in Italy and staying at Lake Como: '*Every day it grows in beauty, and I regret exceedingly leaving it. My dearest wish had been to visit Venice before I turned my steps homewards, as there is a friend there whom I greatly desired to see.*' Who was this friend that Shelley desired to see? What a true wonder woman. I will forever love her.

I feel the same. Ramble on. I must leave or I will become a withered leaf, lifeless and weightless. I shall move on. Ramble on, just like the Led Zeppelin song. And now's the time, the time is now to sing my song.

Yes, I need to move, move on, move about, move around. I must leave, to find the dancing path of my spirit, to feel the freedom that still belongs to me, or to see the shadow of the freedom. But to see the shadow of freedom, I must stand in the sun.

These are the recent words from E. I hope these are not his last words for me, because I am still hoping that our story will continue to unfold, that our words will continue to reach each other. But he has been writing in such a manner that it feels like he is sending me his final message.

'It occurs to me that I don't entirely understand your personal lexicon. Maybe we need to invent another language, a new language. But would a new language suffice? A superabundance of the language that I have for you certainly never will. Perhaps nothing can fill in the great abyss, the ocean that is between us? This book, *Radical*, you must devote yourself to it. It must touch the heart of things.'

尾 / TAIL

When I finally return to New York, E has just left the city. It has been almost two years since our separation. I never imagined that he would leave New York. For me, he and New York are one thing; I could never think of the city without E in it. Yes, this time, New York is different once more. It is not the city I thought I knew. It is again a new place, but with a tiny part of my history in it.

It is to be a brief visit to give two lectures at a college in Manhattan. I stay in a place very close to his old building by the Hudson. The first morning, I walk along the river, recalling the moments when I lived here, with E and without. I walk to the sports complex in Riverside State Park. Over the next two days I give the lectures as planned. In the late afternoons, faces become blurry and jet lag comes upon me. On the last day of my visit, in the afternoon, I walk to Morningside Park. Part of me quietly hopes that, by some strange connection, I might encounter E there. I walk my old route, from the back of the Cathedral of St John the Divine down the steps leading to the park. I do not find the white peacock I once saw. Is it still alive? Peacocks can live for up to forty or fifty years. Might it be lurking nearby in the garden? I walk down into Morningside Park. It is very quiet. One or two joggers pass by. I find my Chinese pond under the cliff. The water is the same muddy green, overgrown with algae. Here the fountain still stands, with the strangely carved faun sculpture under the menacing bear. Nothing has changed.

As I am leaving the park, an unfamiliar sight catches my eye. From a distance, it looks like a large-scale reclining Buddha, though it is painted a greenish blue. As I move closer, a reclining Statue of Liberty reveals itself. It is new. I am astonished. A thinking and reclining Statue of Liberty, without her torch or her upright force! I had not expected this – an image which is not typically American. Is she in repose? What is she thinking? Is she pondering the current state of America? The state of our world?

I take a photo of the statue, and say goodbye to New York. I catch myself thinking about the finality of this 'farewell'. Why should I close myself off from possibility? The future is open. I may return.

Notes and Bibliography

10 Perfume, *'Houses and rooms are full of perfumes . . .'* Walt Whitman, *Leaves of Grass: The First (1855) Edition*, Penguin Books, 2005.

20 Garbanzo Beans, *'America when I was seven momma took me to Communist cell meetings . . .'* Allen Ginsberg, from *Collected Poems: 1947–1980, Allen Ginsberg*, HarperCollins, 1984.

24 Dwell, *'Is God unknown? Does he manifest as the sky? . . .'* 'In lieblicher Bläue' (In Lovely Blue), Friedrich Hölderlin, *Selected Poems and Fragments*, translated by Michael Hamburger, Anvil Press reprint of the 1961 Penguin Books edition.

36 Übermensch, *'I teach you the overman . . .'* Friedrich Nietzsche, *Thus Spoke Zarathustra*, translated by R. J. Hollingdale, Penguin Classics, 1961, reprinted 2003.

53 Crossing Brooklyn Ferry, *'I am with you, you men and women . . .'* Walt Whitman, *Leaves of Grass: The First (1855) Edition*, Penguin Books, 2005.

57 X, *'X is a letter . . .'* Samuel Johnson, *A Dictionary of English Language: An Anthology*, selected and edited by David Crystal, Penguin Books, 2006.

61 Immigration, *'to remove into a country for the purpose of permanent residence . . .'* *Webster's New International Dictionary of the English Language*, G. & C. Merriam Co., 1928.

71 Embalmed Animal, *'animals are divided into . . .'* Jorge Luis Borges, *Selected Non-Fictions*, translated by Eliot Weinberger and Esther Allen, Penguin Books, 2000.

72 Embalmed Animal, *'This [Borges] passage quotes . . .'* Michel Foucault, *The Order of Things: An Archaeology of the Human Sciences*, Tavistock Publications, 1970.

102 Hymen, *'With flowers, garlands, and sweet-smelling herbs . . .'* John Milton, *Paradise Lost*, first published 1667.

104 Spittoon (Sputum) Theory of Womanhood, '*When a man makes love with a woman . . .*' and '*This is the spittoon theory of womanhood . . .*' transcript from D. A. Pennebaker's documentary on Norman Mailer and Germaine Greer's 1971 debate in New York, released in the public domain.

109 Periwinkle, '*There once the walls . .*' Edward Thomas, 'A Tale'. 1917. Reproduced under licence from Faber and Faber Ltd via *First World War Poetry Digital Archive*, http://ww1lit.nsms.ox.ac.uk/ww1lit/collections/item/2854.

132 Heaven is Boundless, Earth is Eternal, '*Heaven is boundless . . .*' Lao Tzu, *Tao Te Ching*, ancient text, rearranged and translated by the author.

136 Flyway, '*I was thinking about the lagoon in Central Park . . .*' J. D. Salinger, *Catcher in the Rye*, Little, Brown, 1951.

142 Scheidekünstler, '*certain chemists who are skilled in the art of . .*' translated by David Constantine, Oxford World Classics, 2008; and '*a title of honour to chemists is to call them artists . . .*' translated by R. J. Hollingdale, Penguin Books, 1978; original text by J. W. von Goethe, 1809.

153 Roots, '*Vitally, the human race is dying . . .*' D. H. Lawrence, *A Propos of Lady Chatterley's Love*, Mandrake Press Ltd, 1930.

156 Flowers, '*The part of a plant which contains the seeds . . .*' Samuel Johnson, *A Dictionary of English Language*, first published 1755.

161 Daisy, '*When daisies pied and violets blue . . .*' William Shakespeare, *Love's Labour's Lost*, c.1590s.

173 Flu, '*You must have this virus . . .*' transcript from *The South Bank Show* of Ingmar Bergman's speech in 1978, released in the public domain.

192 Automobile, '*In the beginning, this happy pedestrian society . . .*' Friedrich Dürrenmatt, *Automobile and Railroad Nations*, translated by Joe Agee, University of Chicago Press, https://press.uchicago.edu/books/durrenmatt/auto_and_railroad.html

216 Witch Hazel, '*The Honeysuckle and the Hazel . . .*' Marie de France, 'The Honeysuckle and the Hazel', a thirteenth-century *lai*, rearranged by the author.

222 The Yellow Peril, '*Whoever will take the time to read . . .*' public speech by Warren Harding, 'Address of the President of the United States on the

Celebration of the Semicentennial Founding of the City of Birmingham, Alabama' (26 October 1921), quoted in Thomas Gossett, *Race: The History of an Idea in America*, Southern Methodist University Press, 1963.

229 Chimonanthus, '*Ode to the Lamei Blossom . . .*' Mao Zedong, public domain, translated by the author.

239 Traumsprache, '*In spite of this indefiniteness . . .*' Sigmund Freud, in *The Pelican Freud Library*, Vol. 1, translated and edited by James Strachey, Penguin Press, 1973.

240 Traumsprache, '*Dreamers of wine drinking often sigh . . .*' Zhuangzi, 'Discourse on All Things Equal', ancient text, translated and rearranged by the author.

243 Mauvais Sang, '*I shall return with limbs of iron . . .*' Arthur Rimbaud, *A Season in Hell*, first published 1873, translation by Norman Cameron, Anvil Press Poetry, 1994.

249 Woodpecker, '*When you are old and grey . . .*' W. B. Yeats, 'When You Are Old', originally published in 1891. *The Collected Poems of W. B. Yeats* (1989), Wordsworth Poetry Library

262 Teignmouth, '*A thing of beauty is a joy for ever . . .*' John Keats, *Endymion*, first published 1818.

266 Minor / Minority, '*How many people today live in a language that is not their own . . .*' Gilles Deleuze and Felix Guattari, *Kafka: Toward a Minor Literature*, 1975, translated by Dana Polan, University of Minnesota Press, 1986.

305 Olga Ivinskaya, '*The clock-face wearily ascending . . .*' Boris Pasternak, *Unique Days*, 1960, Peter Owen Publishers, 1990.

307 Ophelia, '*What of her glass without her . . .*' Dante Gabriel Rossetti, 'Without Her', 1882.

316 Polymath, '*I think of Tai Mountain*', Zhang Heng, 'Four Sorrows', ancient text, translated and rearranged by the author.

329 Ramble On, '*Every day it grows in beauty . . .*' Mary Shelley, *Rambles in Germany and Italy in 1840, 1842, and 1843*, British Library, 2010.

List of Artworks

All artworks and photos have been created by the author.

7   Empire State Building: *night for the empire*
9   The Brooklyn Eagle: *Whitman plaque*
12 Harlem: *Harlem buildings*
15 The Ramble: *in the Ramble*
18 Empty Space: *Chinese character* kong
21 Garbanzo Beans: *Jesus is alive*
23 Soybeans: *New York City*
25 Dwell: *Riverside evening*
27 Hudson River: *crab by the bank*
33 Woman: *Chinese characters for 'women'*
37 Übermensch: *Maison Harlem*
38 The A Train: *St John of Morningside Park*
41 Mother: *oracle bone writing for 'women'*
45 Tribeca: *lady crossing a street*
47 Faun: *faun in Morningside Park*
50 Lebenskünstler: *Harlem housing*
51 Femmes Fatale: *Riverside State Park*
54 Crossing Brooklyn Ferry: *Brooklyn Bridge*
57 X: *pencil sketch after Singer Sargent's* Madame X
62 Immigration: *Avenue of the Americas*
72 Embalmed Animal: *skating park*
73 Erya: *an original page from* Erya
75 Erya: *Chinese character for 'beasts'*
76 Laconic: *125th subway mural*
79 Plantain: *apple of Harlem*
83 Juzi: *orange peel*
88 Carnegie Hall: *fountain*
92 Mandarin: *Chinese slogans*

94 Roget's Thesaurus: *Go board*

99 Frictions: *bedroom window*

105 Spittoon Theory of Womanhood: *Apollo Theater*

108 Periwinkle: *periwinkle mural*

111 Verrazzano-Narrows Bridge: *view of Verrazzano Bridge*

118 Eros vs Aphrodite: *statue in the NYPL*

121 Sugar Plum Fairy: *sign in Grand Central Station*

125 Rattan: *Romeo and Juliet in Central Park*

133 Heaven is Boundless, Earth is Eternal: *Times Square subway*

135 Self-pollinating: *avocado stone*

137 Flyway: *wall with bird*

139 Elective Affinities: *Goethe's book with hair band*

144 Scheidung: divorce: *mural around a window*

152 Divine Farmer: *lake*

157 Azalea Walk: *bush in Central Park*

165 Euphoria: *tree against a painted wall*

168 Camellia: *66th Street*

182 Who's Afraid of the Big Bad Wolf?: *subway exit in NYC*

184 Unoccupied: *Times Square*

188 Bicycle: *Chinese characters for vehicle* – che

192 Automobile: *buffalo eyes*

195 Immobility: *dried flower pods*

199 Zheng He's Navigation Map: *sketches of Zheng's map*

204 Morpheus: *variation on Goya's* The Sleep of Reason Produces Monsters

205 Walking Backwards: *author's parents in Rome*

208 Melancholia: *variation on Arnold Böcklin's* Die Gräberinsel *with an added sun*

214 Soil: *garden snails*

217 Witch Hazel: *Hudson mist*

219 Dialect: *in a Chinese street*

224 Withdraw: *96th Street, Broadway*

229 Chimonanthus: *lamei blossoms*

236 Leitmotiv / Leitmotif: *guitar in shadow*

238 Liebestod – love death: *lamp in the NYPL*

242 Liebesträume: The Peony Pavilion *sketches*

244 Mauvais Sang: *entrance of the Met Opera House*

245 Filling Up, Finish, Full: *the Chinese character 'wan'*

248 Paradox: *hand holding crushed flowers*

254 Wollstonecraft: *statue of Mary Wollstonecraft by Maggi Hambling*

256 Qiu Jin: *framed Qiu Jin above a house plant*

260 St Ives: *beach in England*

265 The Irish Sea: *sea and hills*

269 Coolie: *Central Park, looking south*

270 Grow Your Hair and Keep Your Faith: *the Chinese characters of the phrase*

271 Endurance: *graffiti*

273 Good Herbs Taste Bitter: *ginger*

279 Horticulturist: *fruit bowl*

281 Guerrilla Gardening: *flowers on doors*

282 Bioturbation: *crab against white*

285 Ecofeminism: *lost doll on the beach*

288 Der Kiez: *vase by the window*

293 Taṇhā: *the Chinese characters for* taṇhā

295 Samsara: *the Chinese characters for* samsara

296 Turandot: the Hudson, in the afternoon

298 Drowned: *River Ouse*

302 Yayoi Kusama: *in Kusama's show*

306 Ophelia: *Ophelia above masks*

314 Genji: *facing roses*

317 Polymath: *envelope with a Zhang Heng stamp*

322 Individual: *performance near King's Cross*

325 Big Chill: *winter tree*

332 Tail: *statue in Morningside Park*

Acknowledgements

I want to give a huge thanks to my editor Poppy Hampson for her sharp and sensitive suggestions and Graeme Hall for his meticulous picture editing and overall editorial work. Together they have added immeasurably to the qualities of this narrative-diary, with its etymological flourishes. Becky Hardie and Asia Choudhry also constantly provided me with support. My agent Rebecca Carter and my publisher Clara Farmer are always encouraging.

I want to thank too my American editors at Grove: Amy Hundley, Gretchen Mergenthaler, Deb Seager, Joseph Payne, and of course Morgan Entrekin and my agent PJ Mark. They have been supporting my work for a decade, creating possibilities for the dissemination of my work in the US.

Thank you Kaiya Shang, Dominique Savitri Bonarjee, Philippe Ciompi, Jasmine Marsh, Gareth Evans, Esther Allen, Carol Gluck, Silvia Fehrmann, Stephen Parker, Eoin Dunne, Francisca Monteiro, Katherine Fry, Sally Sargeant and Anne Rademacher.

And of course, Stephen for help with editing and Moon for laughter.